# A Western Horseman Book

*Colorado Springs, Colorado*

# CALF ROPING

## By Roy Cooper

## with Randy Witte

Photographs by Kurt Markus

# CALF ROPING

*Published by*
## The Western Horseman Inc.

3850 North Nevada Ave.
Box 7980
Colorado Springs, CO 80933-7980

*Typography and Production*
**Western Horseman**
Colorado Springs, Colorado

*Printing*
**Williams Printing Inc.**
Colorado Springs, Colorado

*Design*
**Kurt Markus**

*Fourth Printing: June 1991*

ISBN 0-911647-04-X

# DEDICATION

I'd like to dedicate this book to all the people who helped
with my roping career, especially my parents, Tuffy Dale and
Betty Rose Cooper, my wife Lisa, and also to my son Clint. I
hope the book helps others who want to learn the sport.

*Roy Cooper*

ROY COOPER

# CONTENTS

# 1 INTRODUCTION

**Meet Roy Cooper, the man who has changed calf roping standards dramatically since his rookie year in professional rodeo.**

EACH YEAR, for him, is better than the last. He's at the top of his game but hasn't peaked, and there's not even a plateau in sight. He's still climbing, still astounding rodeo fans and contestants, even himself at times, with his ability to rope and win. Summarizing Roy Cooper's achievements in professional rodeo is an on-going endeavor—he has a habit of making and breaking his own records.

In 1983 he was world all-around champion cowboy, world champion calf roper (for the fifth time), even world champion steer roper, an event he admits he never thought about much until a few years ago. He's the first man in 25 years to win three world titles in a single season. Jim Shoulders did it in 1958—all-around, bareback, and bull riding—and won $32,212. Of course the money in pro rodeo has increased substantially since then. Roy Cooper's 1983 total was a new high of $153,391. With bonus earnings like the $25,000 he earned from the Winston Rodeo Series that season, he has become a man of means with a 160-acre ranch near Durant, Okla., and various other investments that will insure a lucrative retirement—if that day ever comes.

Roy Cooper is admired and envied, naturally, but that goes with the territory in any sporting circle. What is important is the fact Roy has achieved all that he has with his ability to rope and tie calves faster than anyone else. And if

*World champion calf roper, steer roper, and all-around cowboy Roy Cooper.*

*Roy, at age 6, learning to tie his first calf at the family ranch near Monument, New Mexico.*

*Roy was 18 when he posed with his dad, Tuffy Dale Cooper, at the conclusion of a matched calf roping benefiting the San Angelo Boys Ranch. The Coopers were matched against their friends, world champion Jim Bob Altizer and his son Mack Altizer. The Coopers won.*

*Roy—in action at the 1983 National Finals Rodeo in Oklahoma City.*
**Photo by James Fain**

he can do it, then someone else may have the opportunity to do it, too, if that someone possesses a similar degree of athletic ability and desire, mental discipline, and a willingness to learn and practice. Roy gives advice freely to aspiring ropers—he loves calf roping, in particular, and wants to have a hand in perpetuating the popularity of the event. He knows the majority of up-and-coming ropers won't approach his level of success, but he'll still tell anyone who wants to learn exactly how he ropes, and why he thinks he wins as often as he does. If the knowledge helps a young roper excel, that's great. That's the purpose of his roping schools, and of this book.

Roy won his first world championship in calf roping in 1976—his rookie year in the PRCA—and his winnings that season came to $43,159. He was the number one roper for the regular season in 1977, with top money of $45,713 altogether, but was declared PRCA champion rather than world champion. The PRCA was in the midst of a three-year trial in which world champions were determined solely by the amount of money won during the National Finals, and Roy

didn't finish first that year at the NFR. The same thing happened in 1978, when he won first again for the PRCA title in calf roping with $67,153 during the regular season.

He suffered a major setback in 1979, sustaining an injury that would have ended the athletic careers of many others. His right hand—his roping hand—was nearly severed when his wrist became entangled in the rope during a practice run. But Roy's perseverance and ambition showed even more clearly when he managed to recover well enough to compete at the National Finals—where he roped with his wrist still stiff, still coupled with surgical pins, and won the NFR average, setting a new record on ten calves of 107.9 seconds.

In 1980 he was calf roping world champion with $77,026 in event earnings. In 1981 his championship total climbed to $94,476; he had the title cinched going into the NFR and finished runner-up for the all-around with $105,814—just $47 behind the number one finisher, his cousin Jimmie Cooper.

In 1982 he entered the Finals in second place, trailing by almost $15,000. By the end of the tenth go-round he had won

*At the 1976 National Finals: Roy won the Rookie of the Year title that season, as well as his first world championship in calf roping.*
**Photo by James Fain**

more than $26,000 in the event, and had taken another world title by a $4,400 margin. By contrast, in 1983 he was so far in the lead for the calf roping crown that he again had the title cinched going into the NFR. He also led for the all-around, and the $20,952 he earned in calf roping, a sum that included yet another NFR average victory, gave him his first all-around championship and set the new money record.

Roy Cooper's debut into pro rodeo wasn't exactly unheralded back in 1976. Stories had circulated for years about how Tuffy Dale Cooper's oldest son was winning it all in the junior rodeos, and later how he was dominating the calf roping on the amateur level. A lot of the top ropers in the PRCA stopped by the Cooper Ranch near Monument, N.M., to lay over between rodeos, and get in a little practice at the ranch arena; and they roped with Roy and watched him and agreed: when his time came to enter the big league of rodeo, he would be tough to beat.

His dad had been more than capable with a rope in his younger days, though he never won a championship. A ranch and family can keep a man fairly close to home, but Tuffy had rodeoed as often as possible, and won a fair share of money in the 1940s and '50s. When the kids came along—Betty Gayle, Roy, and later Clay—Tuffy channeled all his spare time and energy into the role of family calf roping coach. Even wife and mom Betty Rose, a competitive barrel racer and roper herself, joined the family roping sessions. Roy remembers how most every afternoon when he got off the school bus, dad would be waiting down at the arena. Calves were already loaded, horses were already saddled.

Roy purchased a PRCA permit when he was 17, went to one pro rodeo, didn't place, and decided to continue a while longer in the amateur ranks. In 1974, at age 18, he acquired another permit, borrowed his dad's good rope horse, and entered the San Angelo, Tex., rodeo, where he won just over $1,000. The win met requirements for full membership in the association, but Roy waited two years before joining the PRCA tour. His decision to turn pro in 1976 changed calf roping standards dramatically in the years that followed.

Randy Witte

9

# 2 EQUIPMENT

*A good roper stirrup.*

Good equipment, properly fitted to horse and rider, is a necessity for safety and success in calf roping. The saddle should be adequately padded, but still fit close to the horse's back; it should have a moderately low cantle and low saddle horn, but still have good clearance at the gullet so it doesn't put pressure on the horse's withers. Front and back cinches should be of the wide variety so they don't cut into the horse's belly when they're snugged up tight just before you rope. The stirrups should also be of the wide roper type, with plenty of room for your feet to come out of them without hanging up. There are many "roper style" saddles on the market today that have these general specifications. The important thing is to get a saddle that fits you and fits your horse, with the weight distributed evenly on the horse's back.

A rule of thumb for head gear—bits, tie-downs, jerk lines (which we'll cover momentarily)—is to use the minimum amount of equipment necessary to keep a horse working properly. In other words, don't use a severe bit when you don't need it; don't use a severe tie-down if the horse doesn't need it. We're talking in general terms right now; we'll get into specific uses of equipment in the course of the text. The point is, different horses respond to different head gear. Some horses respond well to a bit with a port in it, some prefer a snaffle bit, others work best in a hackamore bit. Whatever the head gear is, it should be sturdy, well balanced, and properly fitted. A bit should be adjusted so the horse grins a little—one wrinkle on each side of his

mouth. The chin strap and bit should take hold when the reins are pulled, and release immediately when the reins are released. You can study the accompanying photographs and see the type of equipment I use. I think it's important to find out what type of bit is best for your horse, because the horse works off the bit in scoring (leaving the roping box just after, but not before, the barrier rope is released), and it is used in stopping, and with the jerk line.

The jerk line is simply a long, soft rope that attaches to the bit, and is run through a pulley or large ring attached to the saddle swell; from there the rope is tucked several times in the roper's belt (as the photographs show). The idea is, when the roper dismounts and heads for the calf during a run, that jerk line will pull out of his belt and tug on the bit, encouraging the horse to stay in a good straight stop, and to take a few steps back. The last tuck of the jerk line should pull free of your belt just before you reach the calf.

You've got to use common sense with this equipment. I don't practice much with jerk lines on my horses, but I use them in competition, and so do most other ropers. A jerk line will encourage a horse to work to the best of his ability; you have to experiment to learn how much pull to use on your horse. A fairly light-mouthed horse probably won't need much pull on the line. And you may want to vary the amount of pull according to the type of calves you're roping. Light calves are best handled when they aren't jerked down—just turned

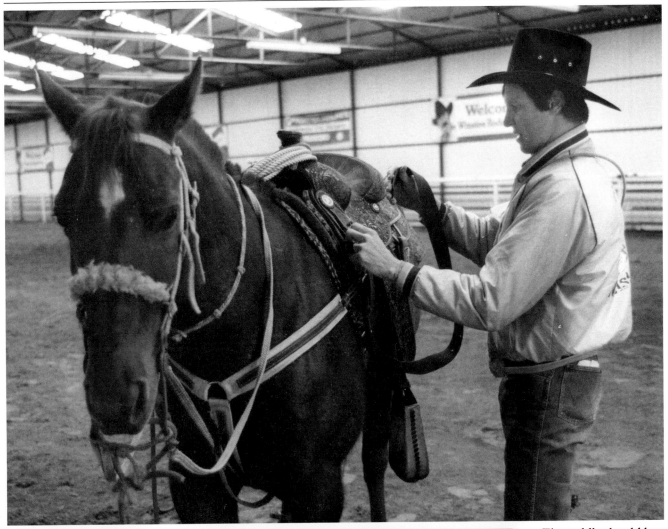

*The saddle should be well padded, but still fit fairly close to the horse's back (above). This will help the horse absorb the jerk on the end of the rope better than a saddle that sits high on his back.*

*My favorite saddle. Note the full-double rigging.*

*The jerk line is rigged, and the long tail is wrapped around the saddle horn—out of the way, but ready for use when it's time to rope.*

*The back cinch attaches to the front cinch under the horse's belly. This prevents the back cinch from slipping farther back to the flank area.*

around. In a case like that, you don't want to have your horse stop exceptionally hard and back up, because the calf probably won't be on his feet when you get to him for the tie.

For big, stout calves, you'll want to encourage the horse to stop and back well. A cross-body pull may be good here. Instead of tucking the jerk line into the left side of your belt, you can tuck it into the right side, so the rope pulls across your body for more friction and a stronger pull.

Other good equipment includes bell boots and skid boots—good insurance for a horse—protecting his legs, preventing him from overreaching and cutting his front legs. Splint boots are a good idea, too, especially for horses that have a tendency to strike an opposite leg. While we're talking about horse gear, I might mention something about the horse, too. A beginner needs a dependable horse, a horse that has been trained for this event, and one that the beginner can handle.

Getting back to what I said about using a minimum of equipment on a horse, here's a tip that will make any rope horse that's high strung easier to handle—*ride*

him. At a lot of my schools, I see students who just saddle their horses and expect to start roping, and they wonder why the horse is high when he's backed in the box. Well, he wants to go, and he hasn't been warmed up, or perhaps we should say ridden down a little. He needs to be loped about five minutes, until his head begins to drop and he starts relaxing. Don't get him hot—after a little loping, if he's still high, walk him around awhile, pen the calves, maybe loosen the cinches and let him stand while you rope a dummy, then ride him some more. If you've got only 30 minutes to rope, rope a dummy, practice tying, or just ride your horse. But don't try to do any calf roping in that length of time.

As for ropes, there is a variety of calf ropes on the market, with numerical designations. Nearly all of them are made out of polyethylene strands, and they're simply referred to as "poly ropes." They've replaced the manila, or "grass ropes," of years gone by. I suggest using a rope 25 or 26 feet long, after it has been attached to the saddle horn.

The lightest ropes are labeled 9.5 or 10.0, and these are generally for young-

12

*Skid boots protect a horse's ankle area on the hind legs when he goes into a hard stop.*

*I like to cut a square hole in the saddle pad, where it goes over the horse's withers, to relieve pressure in that area when the saddle is cinched tightly.*

sters 10 and under, and maybe 10 through 13, respectively. I recommend a 10.5 poly rope for someone between 14 and 18 years of age, and a 10.5 or 11.0 for adults. The ropes get a little heavier and stiffer as the numerals get higher. At any rate, a person needs to experiment, try out a few ropes, see what feels most comfortable to swing and throw. A rope that's a little stiff will make it easier to keep the loop open while you swing it, but it's also tougher to pull the slack out.

A "treated poly" rope is simply a poly that has been treated with a chemical mixture that helps the rope maintain a fairly constant shape and feel, regardless of weather conditions. Synthetic ropes have a tendency to get stiff in hot weather, and limber in cold temperatures.

Another type of rope that I use a lot in competition is a "treated poly-grass rope." This is a sisal rope with a poly core. It has the feel of the old grass ropes, which I grew up using—and really liked—but the strength of poly, which helps prevent it from breaking.

In the old days—up through the mid-1970s—everyone used grass ropes. These were made of high-quality manila

*A wool saddle blanket is placed under the pad.*

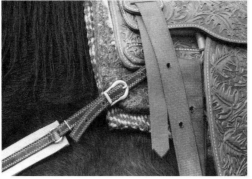

*A variety of breast collars is available, and they attach to or near the top dee ring on each side of the saddle. This piece of equipment helps keep a saddle in place.*

*It's important that a breast collar ride low on the horse's chest, where it won't interfere with his breathing. A middle strap that's run between the front legs and attached to the cinch keeps the breast collar in place.*

*Some horses work better with spurs, some don't. Anyone who wears spurs should know how to ride well enough so the spurs aren't continually bumping the horse. In other words, touch the horse only when it is necessary.*

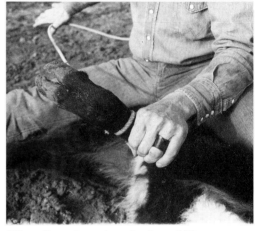

*When I'm tying a lot of calves, I like to wrap a piece of tape on the ring finger of my left hand. This is the finger that can get rope-burned during the final pull while tying a calf.*

*Don't be confused by this metal ring attached to the left rear dee on my saddle. This is where a jerk line is run for steer roping.*

hemp. But the good hemp disappeared—manufacturers quit producing it because it was expensive to make, and there was a steady market for hemp of lesser quality. So that's when U.S. rope makers began experimenting with synthetics.

Some poly ropes have a lot of stretch in them, though, which is bad; it's hard for a horse to continue to work well with a rope that stretches. For actual competition, I like the poly-grass ropes best, but I practice a lot with straight polys, 11.0. For rodeos, I like what is called a treated 93 poly-grass rope. This is slightly heavier than the 11.0 poly, and I can reach for a calf a little better with this type of rope.

You'll also need a couple of piggin' strings—one to carry in your mouth, and a spare tucked under your belt on the right side, out of the way but handy in case you somehow lose the first string during a calf roping run. I nearly always carry two strings in competition—it's good insurance. Most everyone now uses twisted nylon strings, and these come in soft, medium, hard, and various in-between lays (the stiffness factor). A stiff string is harder to handle, but easier to keep the tail out of your wrap. Before I broke my wrist in 1979, I used a stiff string. My wrist is still a little stiff itself since the accident, so now I find it easier to tie with smaller, medium strings, with average lengths of about six feet.

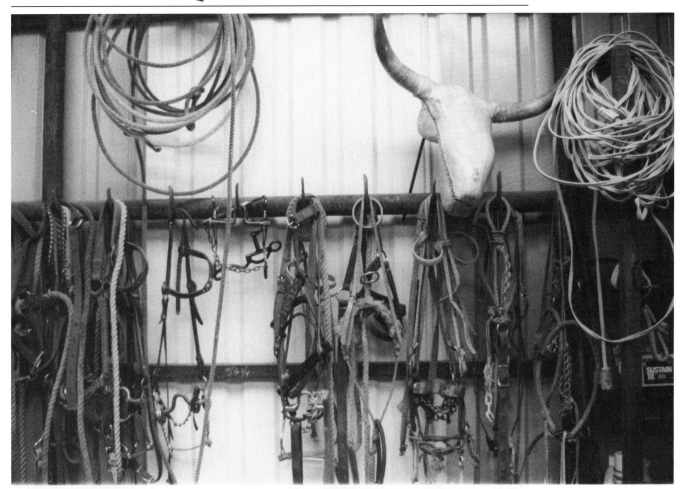

Horses are individuals—a bit that works on one, may not work on another. If a horse seems to have a problem with a bit (fighting it or not working or responding well in it) then try something else. Use the least amount of bit possible—don't use a severe bit if it isn't necessary.

A lot of my horses have worked well in curb bits with fairly high ports. The bit on the left has jointed shanks, and the rubber rings prevent the joints from pinching the horse's lips.

*The bit is properly adjusted in the mouth—not too high, not too low. The horse should "grin" with a wrinkle at each corner of his mouth.*

*A mild tie-down; the sheepskin over the nose helps keep it soft. As it is with bits, the rule applies to tie-downs—don't use a severe tie-down if it isn't necessary.*

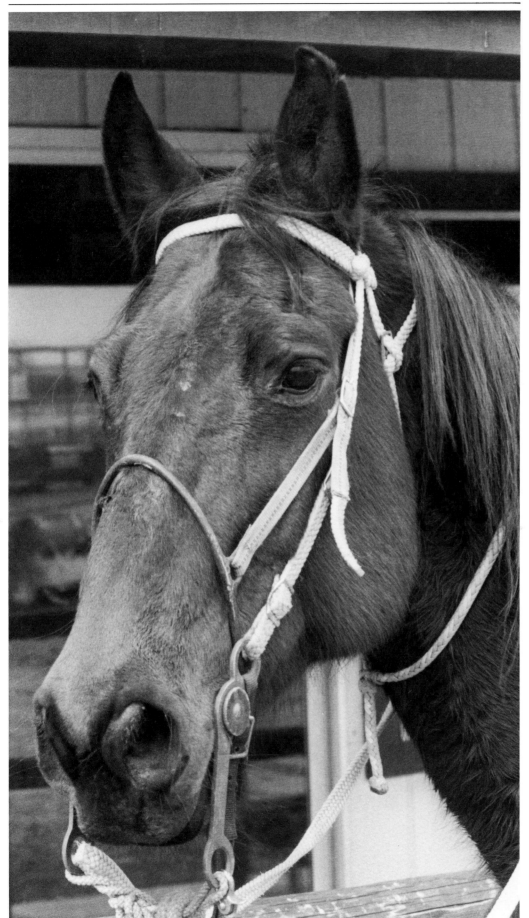

*Another mild tie-down.*

*This horse works best in an iron tie-down. The tie-down helps keep the horse collected, and—along with the bit—aids in the stop by keeping his head down. A horse that throws his head up while stopping won't keep his front feet in the ground, and therefore won't stop well.*

The jerk line is used as an extension of the bridle reins, to encourage the horse to back up as the contestant runs down the rope to the calf.

*The jerk line can be tucked under the belt on the left side or right side. The right side will pull across the body for a stronger pull on the reins, which in turn gets a faster, stronger back-up from the horse.*

The jerk line attaches to the bridle bit, and is run through a pulley connected to the saddle before it is tucked into the roper's belt.

A jerk line may also be run through a metal ring on the saddle, rather than a pulley.

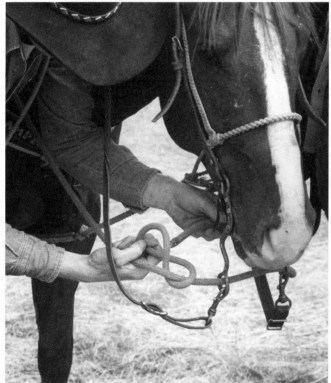

Attaching the jerk line to the bit. . . .

*Rope cans or rope bags will protect your ropes while they're packed for storage or traveling.*

*I prefer rawhide burners on my ropes—they make it easier to pull the slack. But they also wear out a rope more quickly than the leather burners do.*

*Most everyone who has been involved with roping for any length of time winds up with a variety of ropes on hand.*

*The rope—or ropes if you're carrying two loops—should be attached to the base of the saddle horn. The first loop goes on the bottom, and the spare loop goes on top of that. The whole idea is to keep the jerk of the calf as close to the horse's back as possible—it's easier on the horse.*

22

Having good equipment builds confidence. You don't have to worry about something breaking or not working properly. All you have to concentrate on is roping.

*A stout keeper on the end of the rope makes it easy to attach or remove the rope from the saddle horn.*

*Note the pigging string tucked under the belt. One little tuck will hold it in place, but it can be jerked free easily when it's time to make the tie.*

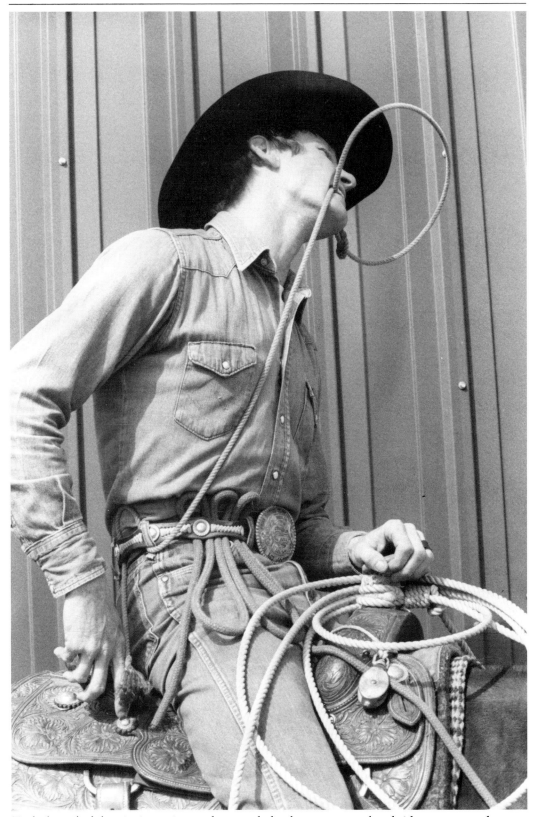

*Tuck the tail of the pigging string under your belt, then turn your head sideways, to make sure there is enough slack in the string to prevent it from being jerked from your mouth while roping or running to the calf.*

*Ready to rope.*

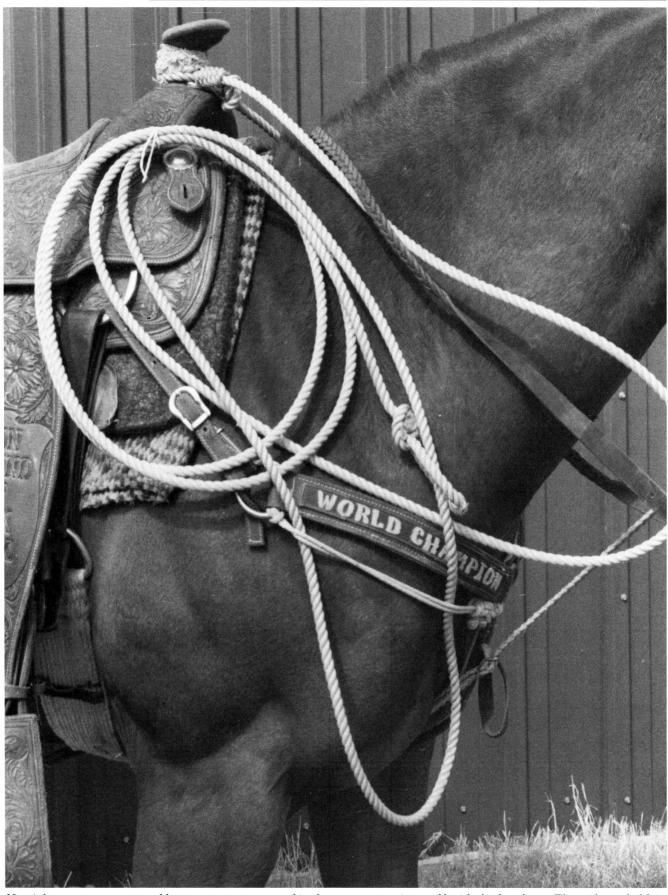

*Here's how to carry a second loop—a spare rope used in the event you miss a calf with the first loop. The coils are held in place with a piece of string attached to a small ring mounted to the side of the gullet. And the loop, already built, slips under the cord attached to the breast collar. Jerk the rope free, breaking the string, and you're ready for another throw.*

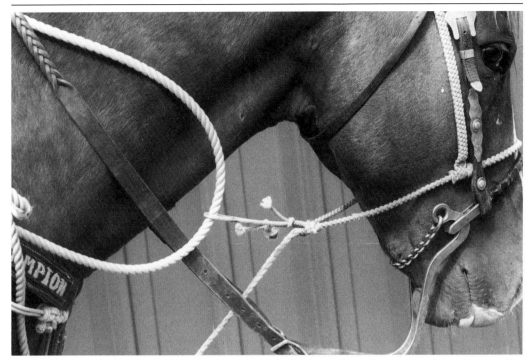

If you've got only 30 minutes to rope, rope a dummy, practice tying, or just ride your horse. But don't try to do any calf roping in that length of time.

*The spare rope doesn't go under a neck rope, as the first one does, but passes through a small loop attached to the tie-down. The spare won't interfere with the first rope in this manner, but because it passes through that small loop in the tie-down, the horse will be kept straight with a roped calf.*

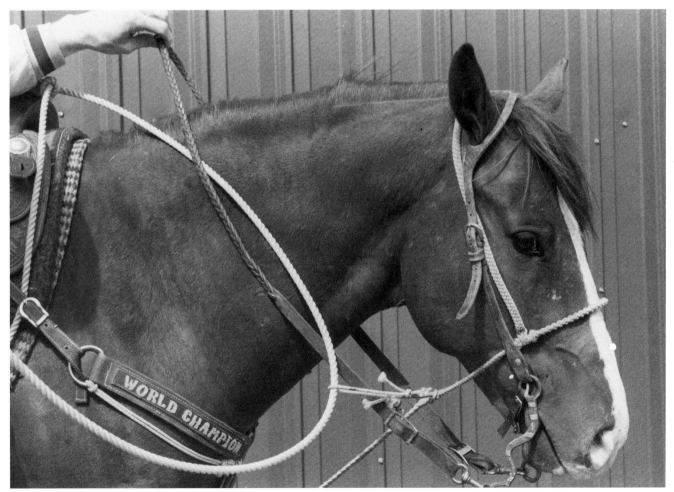

*Make sure your rope—or ropes—pass through the bridle reins. This will prevent the rope from getting caught under the bit and interfering with the horse's work—once a calf is roped.*

# 3 THROWING THE ROPE

**While the ideal position for roping a calf is straight behind, maybe five feet, I think it's important to practice roping a dummy from different angles and distances.**

Beginners need to learn at least a couple aspects of calf roping separately. They need to learn basic rope handling—swinging and throwing the loop—from the ground. And they should be able to ride a horse well enough initially that they don't have to think about horsemanship the whole time when they start roping in the arena. When I was a little kid, my dad started me roping a bucket filled with sand, and I still think this is a good way to begin.

Stand five or six steps behind the bucket; practice building a loop, swinging it and catching the bucket, running up a couple steps as you throw. We'll talk about getting some "dip" in the front of the rope, but don't worry about that initially. Just swing a flat loop over your head, and try to rotate your elbow upward a bit with each swing, as you see me do in the sequence of photographs. Swing at a constant speed, and practice a smooth release with plenty of follow-through, extending your arm toward the target when you release the loop, with fingers pointing toward the target. When the loop settles around the target, let your fingers settle firmly around the rope, palm down; then quickly pull the slack down. Your arm will move almost in an arc—down and back; then you immediately reverse the arc, moving your arm rapidly upward as you pitch the slack forward and high in the air and release it.

From the bucket you can graduate to a regular dummy. I like a dummy calf head, stuck in a bale of hay, because the view is similar to that of a real calf.

When you reach this stage of practice, think about getting a little dip in the front of that loop, as the photographs show. You get this dip with more elbow and wrist action, and by moving in to the target, increasing the downward angle of your loop as it swings. This dip is vital in calf roping, because it makes the loop curl upward, behind the calf's head; a loop that doesn't curl could catch a front foot as well as the head. That's a bad catch that sets up a difficult tie. You want a smooth, rapid swing; don't slow down the loop just before you throw—keep it going at the same rate of speed. Run up to the dummy and strive for a quick release, extending your arm and fingers for good follow-through. Then rip the slack out and pitch it high.

You can hold one or two coils of rope in your other hand; it really doesn't matter, just whatever you find you can handle best. I do it both ways. Notice, though, how high and how close I hold my coils to the hand I'm roping with. This is the same position you'll have your hands in when you rope from a horse.

While the ideal position for roping a calf is straight behind, maybe five feet, I think it's important to practice roping a dummy from different angles and different distances. In competition, you won't always have a perfect throw. For a chance at winning, you might have to throw at an angle, or "reach" for a hard-running calf. If you've practiced throwing from different positions, you'll be ready to adapt to different conditions that arise in the arena. The whole idea of

Here's the dip in the front of the loop. The dip comes from increased action in the wrist and elbow—the elbow rotates upward with each swing. The angle at which the rope swings will vary according to the distance to the calf's head; a sharp downward angle is necessary for a close catch, but the angle decreases the farther behind the roper is from his target.

The arm also moves slightly forward and backward while swinging the loop; and the wrist rolls back and forth, up and down, with each swing. The first finger on the right hand is extended to help keep the loop open, and to give the final measure of control over the loop as it swings, and as it is thrown.

Hold one coil or two, whichever feels best.

Hold the coils high, simulating the position the rope would be held on horseback.

And concentrate on the target. Eyes should be focused on the back of the calf's head.

*For a practice dummy, I like the plastic calf head—because the view is similar to what you see when roping a real calf.*

*The dummy has a couple metal rods in the neck. Turn a bale of hay on edge, stick the dummy in one end of it, and you're ready to practice.*

31

*Another view of the swing.*

*Look at my hand and elbow.*

*I'm moving up a couple steps—good practice for when I'm roping a calf "going to him," rather than rating him.*

*I've taken the second step, and this swing will deliver the loop.*

*The throw. . . .*

*And the catch. Notice the figure-eight that forms.*

practicing is to train your muscles, your reactions. When calf roping times are running around eight or nine seconds, there obviously isn't much time for thinking. It's all reaction. That's the way I rope. My mind and muscles automatically react to the situation at hand. I've developed that ability through a lot of practice all the years I was growing, building on whatever God-given talent I have.

And I think a person's mental attitude during practice makes all the difference in obtaining the most from those sessions. I went through a phase a few years ago when I went to the practice pen just because I knew I had to practice, had to put in my time. I got out of that habit when I started thinking back to the practice sessions we had when I was growing up. I was always working on solving specific problems in those days, or working to obtain specific goals. So that's the way I practice. I practice to win—to be a better roper tomorrow than I am today.

Okay, so you're practicing roping the dummy. You're beginning to feel comfortable with a rope in your hands; you're throwing hard with plenty of fol-

low-through, making catches, ripping the slack out and pitching it straight up. Now, here's something else to try—try feeding the loop, starting with a slightly smaller loop in your hand than you want to throw. Not every great calf roper through the years has fed his loop—that is, slipped a little extra rope in the loop before he threw it. But most of the ropers do this. I like to start with a smaller loop because I feel I can get it up and swinging faster. Actually, I make one swing and then feed, and I'm ready to catch from that point on. I can catch on the second swing if the opportunity is there.

You feed a loop by learning to let a little tail slip through your hand while swinging. This extra rope comes from between your hands. The centrifugal force of the loop moving around your head will pull whatever additional rope you want into the loop. And again, this is a personal factor. You use a fairly small loop for roping calves. You can study the photographs and try to pattern your loop after mine, but it all boils down to whatever size loop you learn to feel most comfortable with, whatever you can handle.

*Feeding the loop: Here's the size loop I start with (top), and the size I end up with after I've fed it.*

*Swing the loop; when you're ready to throw, take two steps. Start on the right foot, and throw on the second step.*

*It's also a good idea to practice roping from a stationary spot behind the dummy. This simulates roping a calf while your horse is rating him, maintaining a constant distance behind. Here's the final swing and the throw. . . .*

*And here's the catch. The loop curls up and back, forming the figure-eight. The loop will curl back like that if it's thrown hard— has plenty of zip on it. And the curl prevents a front leg from being caught along with the head.*

*Pull the slack, and then pitch it forward, straight and high.*

*Practice really ripping the slack out with a strong, fast pull.*    *Then shoot it up.*

*Get into rhythmn with your swing when you practice stepping toward the dummy. Swing and step, right and left.*

*The second step is bigger than the first. A left-handed roper would step left, then right. Remember to follow through on the throw. My right hand continues to point to the head after the loop has been released.*

*As soon as the rope curls back, it's time to pull the slack.*

*Take a step back, and this will simulate the horse stopping as the calf continues to run.*

*You can practice roping a dummy from horseback, too. Position the horse as if he were rating the calf.*

*And you can practice the dismount. Throw the slack and tag the horse, dismounting low over his hindquarters.*

*The right hand should push straight down— not to the side—when tagging the horse. And the roper should stay close to the horse as he steps off.*

*Stay away from the horse's face as you start down the rope.*

# 4 FLANKING & LEGGING

**Lift straight up and use your hands and body to roll the calf in the air, so he lands flat on his left side with legs extended.**

There is more basic ground work ahead. Roping is an essential part of this event, of course, but once the calf is caught, the difference between winning and losing lies in getting from horse to calf, and in efficient flanking and tying. Let's talk about flanking, first.

There is no substitute for a real calf when it comes to practicing flanking. A good way to do this is to take an old rope, tie it around a calf's neck with a knot that won't slip, making sure he can breathe easily; and tie the other end of the rope to a post. The calf should be standing in ground that has been worked up, so it is soft. Now you can practice running down the rope with your left hand over the rope, and flanking. Here's what you do:

Think about forward motion—everything connected with calf roping is forward motion for the roper. Run down the rope fast and low like a sprinter, leaning forward, springing off your toes, reaching for the calf. Let your left hand follow the rope down to the calf's head as you move your left leg into the calf's shoulder. Your left knee will block the calf and prevent him from moving forward. Lift with your left hand to keep his head up. At the same time lean and reach forward with your right hand, over the back, so you can grab the flank.

Don't waste time trying to "get set" to lift the calf off the ground—make it one flowing motion. When you first make contact with the calf with your left hand and leg, and almost simultaneously with your right hand, you should be coming up from underneath the calf with your right thigh—one smooth motion. Lift

him straight up in the air, so his legs just clear the ground. Don't step forward; don't take a step back. Lift straight up and use your hands and body to roll the calf in the air, so he lands flat on his left side with legs extended.

If the calf is jumping up and down when you reach him, that's fine; get in time with his upward motion as you lift, and the flanking will be easier. Ideally, when you're actually roping and a calf is jerked down, you want to get to him just as he's getting up, so you can flank him when he takes that first jump. This saves time, because the calf is helping you flank him.

So that's flanking, basically. We'll get into tying in a moment, but as long as we're discussing getting calves on the ground, we should explain the method of legging a calf down.

When my dad started roping, legging was often *the best* way to get a calf on the ground. The calves were usually bigger back then, and sometimes wilder, with a lot of rank, lanky Brahmas or Brahma-crosses at the rodeos, and legging a calf down was the best method for handling cattle like that. Youngsters, of course, will have to leg calves down until they're big enough to handle flanking. I legged calves into my teens and won a lot of junior rodeos doing this.

Without getting too far ahead of ourselves, I should point out that most everyone these days gets off the horse on the right side to save time—you don't have to cross under the rope, as you do on a left-side dismount. A right-handed roper who knows in advance that he will want to leg a calf down, rather than

41

flank him, can dismount from either side, but the left is probably a little faster. From the left, you go straight down the rope, leg the calf down, step over him, and you're ready to tie.

Say you're legging down a calf after a dismount to the left. You run down the rope, with your right hand following the rope to the calf's head, as in flanking. But when you get to the calf's shoulder, you reach down with your left hand and grab his right front leg just below the elbow. Stay in close to the calf's shoulder with your right leg—if the calf jumps, he won't get away, and in fact the jump will make it easier to throw him. When you've got a firm grip with your left hand, bring your right hand to the calf's leg, between his knee and fetlock, and step close to his side as you lift him off his feet and push him down on his side.

The procedure is the same on a right-side dismount—you're just switching roles with your hands. And you've got to roll the calf over to his other side before you step across and string. Legging should be one continuous movement, as it is with every aspect of calf roping.

Incidentally, the PRCA judges are particular about seeing "daylight" under a calf whether you're flanking or legging, meaning that the calf must be lifted so his feet are clearly off the ground. You can't just try to knock a calf down or push him over. However, if a calf is jumping in the air when you first lay hands on him—and you're in proper position—you can go ahead and tip him for the fall in mid-air without allowing his feet to touch the ground first.

*Here's the proper position to be in for flanking. The roper should stay low over the calf's back; the right hand grasps the flank area while the right leg moves under the calf's belly to come up and help with the lift.*

You can't just try to knock a calf down or push him over.

*The left hand is lifting on the rope; the left leg blocks the calf and prevents him from jumping forward. Assistant Johnny Mann holds the calf's tail—a standard procedure during a practice session for flanking and tying.*

1/ Block him off and reach. . . .

2/ Then go straight up with the calf. Don't step forward or backward. Roll the calf on his side while he's off the ground.

*3/ The release.*

*4/ Grab the calf's front leg as he lands, then step across and string. My right hand is reaching for the string in my mouth as my right foot begins to take the step.*

1/ To leg a calf, block him off with your right leg, then reach for his right front leg.

2/ After you've got a good hold on the leg, shift to the side.

3/ And then grasp the leg with your right hand.

4/ Lift the calf up. . . .

Youngsters will have to leg calves down until they're big enough to handle flanking. I legged calves into my teens and won a lot of junior rodeos doing this.

*5/ And push him to his side.*

*6/ Step toward the calf as he lands.*

*7/ Then step across, maintaining your grip on his leg.*

8/ Now you're in position to make the tie, the same as if you had flanked the calf down.

Another view of the flanking procedure.

9/ The tail of the pigging string should land four or five inches in front of the hind legs, and my right hand will be free to gather both hind feet.

# TYING

**If you tie close to the ground, the calf is less likely to kick.**

The most important part of tying has to do with positioning the calf's feet. At my roping schools, we have tying drills in which I count cadence; we go through the tie step-by-step: "Ready one!" Pull the calf's top front foot into position, place the piggin' string right above the fetlock, and pull the loop tight *as you simultaneously step across the calf with your right foot.* Step and string in *one motion.* Study the sequence of photographs carefully and try to duplicate the positions.

"Ready two!" Throw the tail of the string to the side at the angle you see in the photograph, so it lays about four or five inches in front of the hind feet, then reach down with your right hand and grab the lower hind foot. Roll your wrist up to cross the feet as you bring them up to, and on top of, the front foot. Hold the legs in position with your right leg. Look at my body position—I'm above the calf, leaned over; I maintain this position throughout the tie. Notice also that the calf's feet meet right in the middle of his body. My right elbow is out, my chin is tucked, my eyes are on the

*You can use one, two, or three wraps and a hooey. I usually use two. One wrap is risky—the calf might kick free.*

50

feet. I'm pulling with my left hand to keep his front foot in position, and I'm applying pressure with my right thigh to keep his back feet in position.

"Ready three!" Reach down and pick up the string.

"Ready four!" Complete the tie. I use a short wrap—two wraps and a hooey. The traditional tie is three wraps and a hooey, but I get along okay with two wraps, and this saves time.

I think it's important to tie fairly close to the ground. A lot of people have a tendency to roll the calf on his back, with his feet sticking high in the air, and this is what makes a lot of calves kick. If you tie closer to the ground, the calf is less likely to kick. Tie all three legs with a tight first wrap, and then a second; your left hand is still holding the front leg, and when the right hand is passing by again for the hooey, release the leg with your left hand to hold the string. Bring the tail of the string through the V with your right hand, and pass it to your left. The fingers on your left hand reach up through the V to bring the string down into a half-hitch.

The V is formed between the crossed feet—between the front foot and the back feet. The left-hand fingers are on top of the first two wraps, and under the hooey wrap, which is brought around the front foot, through the V to the left hand, and pulled tight. This forms the half-hitch, or hooey in the string. Use both hands to make this final pull. It doesn't matter whether you pull the tail of the piggin' string completely through the hooey or not—just make sure the wraps and half-hitch are tight.

My right hand travels in a relatively small circumference, circling the feet with the string, and I keep the upper part of my body leaned over. This body position, over the calf, will feel awkward at first, but once you condition your muscles to it, it is by far the most efficient position for tying. Start slowly, step by

(Continued on page 56)

1/ The calf has just been flanked. I'm stepping across with my right leg as I place the loop on the pigging string on the calf's top front leg.

2/ The loop has been pulled tight, and the tail tossed to the side. My right hand scoops up the hind feet.

*3/ The back feet are placed over the front foot, and my right hand moves to the tail of the string to begin the wrap.*

*4/ One wrap is on, and I'm putting on the second wrap. My right leg continues to hold the back feet in place.*

5/ It's important to keep your elbow up throughout the tie.

6/ I'm putting three wraps on this one.

7/ My left hand continues to hold the calf's front leg in place.

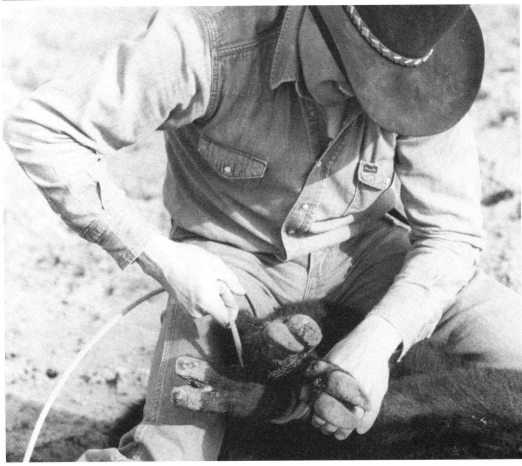

8/ My left hand moves to the string and holds it firmly as I come up with the string to complete the final wrap.

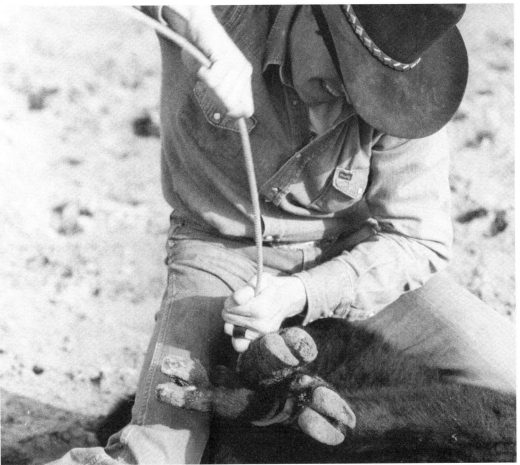

**9/** *This time my right hand brings the string on top of the front leg—through "the V"—as my left hand reaches through the loop (formed by the last wrap), and pulls the string on through.*

**10/** *I use both hands to pull the string tight, completing the tie.*

*Body position is important—work directly above the calf. The strain is on your right leg. This is an awkward position to assume, at first, but your muscles will gradually get conditioned to it.*

step with the cadence. The speed will come naturally with practice. If you develop good habits in the beginning, you'll react properly with speed at a rodeo, when that time comes. When you practice, practice first on tying correctly, tying the feet close to the ground with the front leg and back legs placed evenly in the middle of the calf's body. Then, later, practice for speed and tying tightly.

Now study the sequence of photographs in which I use a two-handed tie. By two-handed tie, I mean I use my left hand to help my right hand pull the tail on each wrap for good tight wraps. A two-handed tie is used whenever something goes wrong, like putting the loop over my hand on the front foot, or stringing a dew claw, or when a calf is straining or kicking. If any of these things occur, I automatically go into my two-handed tie. Getting back to accidentally placing the loop over my hand—I don't attempt to move my left hand, or reposition the loop. I go ahead and complete the first wrap, then slip my hand out of the string as I begin the second wrap. It's at that point that I go into the two-handed tie. I'll even go into the two-handed tie for extra security—to make absolutely certain the calf doesn't kick free—if I've got plenty of time to win the average on my last calf. Sometimes, with a kicking or straining calf, you find that you just can't get both hind feet up in position together. If that happens, go ahead and concentrate on bringing up the bottom hind foot and getting a wrap on it. Then bring the other foot into position for another wrap, continuing the two-handed tie. We'll get into more of these "What if?" categories, and you'll see more two-handed ties, in the chapter on "Problem Calves, Problem Catches, Problem Horses."

Now, what about one wrap and a hooey?

You've probably seen calf ropers gam-

ble with this, trying to save a little time. I don't recommend this tie for beginners, because it isn't a secure tie; like I said, it's a gamble. I've won a lot of money with one wrap and a hooey, and I've also lost a lot of money because of it, when the calf kicked free. All I can say is, when it's necessary and it works, it's fine. But I don't like to be in a position where I have to be so fast that I'm willing to gamble that the calf won't kick free, because I don't think there is more than two- or three-fifths of a second difference between the one wrap and the two wraps. One thing that will make this wrap more secure is to roll the calf over as you complete the tie (using your hands on the string and your right leg, just as you raise up to signal for time). When the calf is rolled over, he can't get his free front foot under him in an attempt to stand, thus taking away his incentive to struggle. But here again, this last little maneuver also takes a fraction of a second, so you might not be gaining much with the one wrap.

The way in which you signal for time is also important. When the tie is complete, throw your hands up high in the air or straight out to the side as you stand. "Daylight" yourself; leave no doubt in the flagger's mind that your run is complete. A good flagger won't drop the flag until he is certain the roper has signalled for time. A roper who casually drops his hands to the side, signalling for time, may cause a little hesitation in the mind of the flagger.

*1/ Here's a close look at the hooey. My left hand holds the final wrap.*

*2/ The string is brought through "the V" and my left hand reaches through to grab it.*

*3/ And the string is pulled tight. It doesn't matter whether the tail is pulled completely through, just as long as the string is pulled tight.*

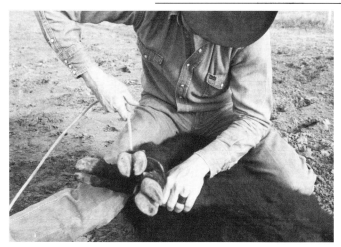

1/ Now let's look at the two-handed tie, which is used to put on extra tight wraps (on a straining calf, for example). I'm putting on the second wrap. . . .

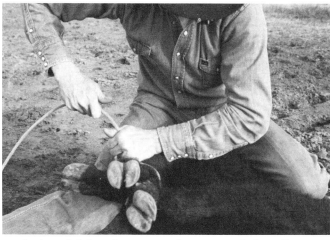

2/ And my left hand moves to the string to help pull it tight. I'll put on three wraps.

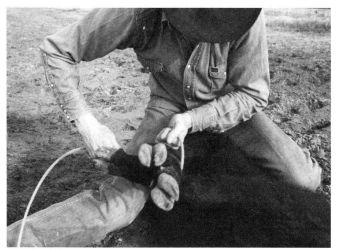

3/ The left hand pulls on the string. . . .

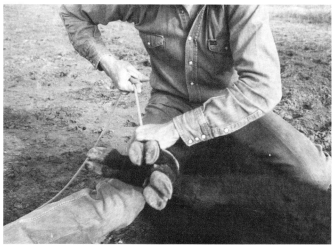

4/ Then goes back for another hold.

5/ The right hand continues the wrap. . . .

6/ Then cuts through "the V."

*7/ I reach through for the pull.*

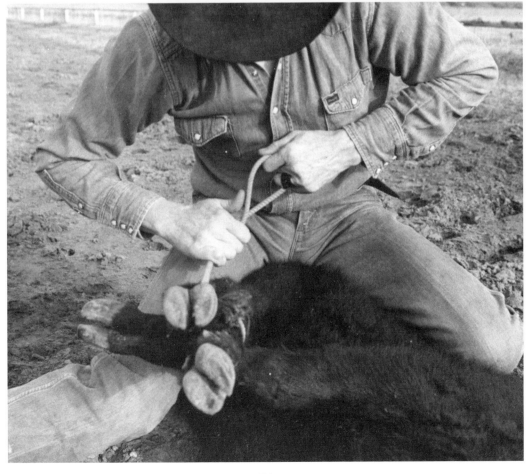

*8/ And it's tight.*

1/ *A photo sequence depicting flanking and tying. . . .*

2/ *Block him off and reach.*

3/ *The right leg moves under the calf.*

4/ *Lift straight up.*

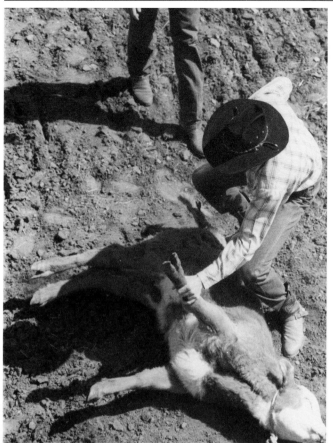

5/ Step and string . . .

6/ . . . in one motion.

7/ Pull the loop tight . . .

8/ . . . then toss it away.

*9/ Gather the hind feet.*

*10/ Place the feet uniformly in the middle of the calf's body.*

*11/ And maintain pressure with right leg and left hand to hold the feet in place.*

*12/ Begin the tie.*

*13/ This is the second wrap.*

*14/ Now for the hooey.*

*15/ Raise up . . .*

*16/ . . . signalling for time.*

# 6 CONSIDER THE ROPE HORSE

*At his indoor arena, Roy has a phone to his ear while he brushes a horse and prepares for a session of roping.*

Anyone who wants to learn to rope has got to have a rope horse, a horse that has been trained for this event. There are plenty of rope horse trainers scattered around the country, and there are plenty of horses for sale in a variety of price ranges.

I was lucky growing up, in that my dad always kept several horses for each of us kids. I started roping on a Welsh pony; I had another horse, later, that had navicular disease. He couldn't be hauled or worked real hard, but he was great for a kid who was learning. He could catch a calf and work a rope. I progressed to bigger, better horses as my horsemanship and roping ability improved. It takes good horses to win.

When you're looking at a prospective horse, have the owner rope on him, then you ride him. Learn all you can about the horse and about the equipment he is used to working with, then decide if that horse is what you want.

As a preface to the next chapter, which deals with roping from a horse, it might be well to discuss some general guidelines on horse care, and point out that rope horses are highly tractable animals, with special needs. For one thing, a rope horse needs a little variety in life. He'll quit working if he doesn't do anything but go from one rodeo to the next throughout the year. What I like to do ideally is to haul one of my horses for a couple weeks, then bring him home and give him a couple weeks away from roping. I change horses a lot. A person with one horse might rope for several days in a row, then just ride for another day; rope some more, and maybe give the horse a day off once a week.

I think it's important for horses to be in good physical condition. I feed oats and a handful of Calf Manna twice a day; I feed a lot of grass hay and a little alfalfa, and I worm my horses every 60 days. When they're home, they have time in a large paddock "just to be horses," but I also see to it that they have exercise. In the summer, they'll be taken for a swim two or three times a week. We have a pond, and the horses will be ridden into it bareback so they can swim for a minute; they'll be brought out and maybe trotted for 30 yards, then go back in the water for another swim. Other days, they'll just be taken for a ride in the evenings, when it's cool. And once a week they'll be sprinted down the arena; sprinted twice that day, once a week.

A person needs to know his horse, or horses, and figure out what schedule best meets the needs of each individual. It boils down to a combination of roping, exercise away from roping, and good care.

When you're ready to go rope, spend time warming up your horse—walking, trotting, loping in circles. Make sure the horse's muscles are warmed up and that he is responsive to you. When you practice, spend time walking him in the box and relaxing. Maybe get off and loosen the cinches for awhile. Score some calves on him—that is, rope a few calves, then turn one out; don't rope, just hold him in the box. The horse will be more responsive and more relaxed when he knows he doesn't *always* have to run out of the box.

A horse that's rodeoing hard will get tired the same as a cowboy. He doesn't get that way from the actual roping; it's

*It takes good horses to win, and good care to keep them that way.*

the hauling that really wears on him. One thing that helps is to have some extra padding in the trailer, under the floor mats. I use heavy rubber mats on top of a couple inches of foam rubber, and this helps lessen the impact of bumps on rough roads. A regular feeding schedule, twice-a-day feedings at regular intervals, also helps keep a horse mentally and physically fit. A feeding schedule is tough to maintain when a guy is rodeoing hard, but I try to stick to the schedule as closely as possible when I'm hauling a horse.

If a horse is well cared for, used regularly but not over-worked, he'll last for years. There are a lot of 15- and 16-year-old horses that are among the very best in professional rodeo.

*A horse needs to be warmed up properly before he goes to work.*

65

# 7 PUTTING IT TOGETHER

*Here's how I hold my reins.*

When I go to the practice pen, I know in the back of my mind that the most important run I'll make that day will be my first run. It's the first run that comes closest to simulating actual rodeo competition, because no one has a chance to make a few practice runs at a rodeo before he ropes for the money. When I back into that box at a rodeo, I want to be prepared to do everything right—*the first time.* I also know that practice won't help me become a perfect roper unless I try to practice perfectly.

So I'll spend time warming up my horse and myself, just like I do before roping in competition. I'll check my equipment; I'll groom my horse. When I saddle, I'll make sure everything is adjusted properly. Then I'll ride out and pen the calves, and take plenty of time warming up my horse—walking, trotting, loping in circles, both directions. I may loosen the cinches and let him stand for awhile, while I rope a dummy or practice flanking and tying, but when I finally back into that box for the first run, I want it to be a good one. I want to be ready to rope, to really have it on my mind.

I'll shake out the size loop I want to start with, before the loop is fed, then walk the horse in the box, turn toward the calf and back up. I'll help the horse pick a spot close to the back of the box, where he's comfortable standing, and can get a good start. I don't want to pull him too tightly into the corner, where he's hunched up in an awkward position, but I do like to quarter a horse in the corner farthest from the calf chute. By that I mean I turn him sideways at about a 45-

degree angle. I feel I have more control, and can judge the barrier best, in this position. I don't practice with a barrier rope—seems like no one does, because it's a hassle to set up the barrier before each run—but I rope like there is a barrier there. I know how far I want to let the calf move—maybe when his shoulder is to the gate after it opens.

As I'm riding into the box, I'll tuck the loop under my right arm, and hold the saddle horn with my right hand, which is also holding the loop. My left hand holds the coils and reins, as the photos show. When the horse is set, I like to

*The ring finger goes between the reins.*

glance down his right side, to make sure he's standing squarely, then I lean forward with my toes pointing downward in the stirrups and my thighs gripping the saddle. I'll watch the calf, and when he's standing squarely with his head up, ready for a good start, I'll nod to the gateman to open the gate.

Well, I'm ready. I nod to the gateman, the calf moves, my horse and I move, and I bring the rope up for the first swing. Two more swings and I throw; the loop settles around the calf's neck and curls upward. I pull my slack and pitch it straight up in the air, then my right hand moves to "tag" the horse on his neck as my left hand pulls the reins to the saddle horn. My left hand then releases the reins as I begin a right-sided dismount, and the calf comes to the end of the rope. My horse is into a good stop when I step off over the hindquarters, then run down the rope. My left arm and hand follow the rope up to the calf's head and neck as my left leg blocks his left shoulder. I lean forward, reaching for the right flank with my right hand, and come up under the calf at the same time. The calf is flanked, I grab his right front leg and have the string on his foot as he hits the ground; the back legs are gathered, I give him two wraps and a hooey, and throw my hands in the air.

What was I, eight or nine seconds?

Let's go through that run again and slow it down, to see what really happened. There are a lot of little steps to go through during a run, but it's basically one continuous motion. One step blends into another.

When I start, I'll use the saddle horn to pull myself forward and up out of the saddle, so I'm moving with the horse, not hindering his start, or mine for that matter. Then I'll bring my loop up for the first swing as the horse leaves the box. I feed my loop on the first swing and I'm ready to catch on the second swing, if the opportunity is there.

When I'm chasing a calf, I'm focusing on his head and trying to get fairly close behind him. I'm also leaning forward and looking around the horse's head—I can see the calf better this way, rather than trying to look over the horse's head, which is the traditional method of roping. The distance from horse to calf will vary as conditions vary from run to

*You can control the horse and the coils in one hand.*

*This is what my left hand looks like when I'm in the box, ready to rope.*

1/ Ready to rope. I'll swing the loop a few times and build the loop I want to start with.

2/ Walk into the box.

3/ And head for the far corner.

4/ The horse is turned toward the calf and backed into the corner as I swing the loop up under my arm and hold it.

5/ I want the horse to be quiet and attentive. As soon as the calf is standing squarely, I'll nod for the gate.

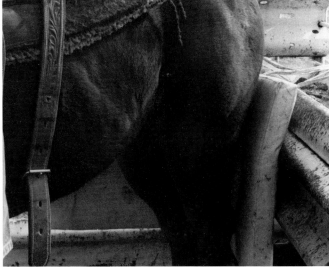

6/ A padded corner in the box will protect the horse from banging into it when he backs.

*7/ When we start, I'll lean forward and catch the saddle horn with my right hand.*

*8/ Toes are pointing down.*

*9/ Note also that the jerk line in this instance runs on the left side, even though I'll dismount to the right—another way to help keep the horse stopping and backing straight.*

*10/ Another view of the start. My rein hand moves forward, signalling the horse to move out.*

*I don't rope at home with a barrier rigged up, but I practice like one is there. I'll let the calf move, then I'll move.*

*My rope comes up.*

*And I'm out of the box.*

run, but it's something like five feet, ideally. Sometimes you might even run up to a calf and bump him, then back off and maintain the distance you were striving for in the first place. The ideal throw comes from straight behind the calf, with the horse rating the calf—maintaining the proper distance for a good catch. When I'm confident of catching, I'll make my throw, focusing on the calf's head, and I'll follow through with my arm and hand, my fingers pointing to the target. When I see the loop settle around the head and curl upward, my right hand will settle around the rope again and I'll pull the slack. The motion is down and back; it's a fast, hard pull, but a smooth motion. A little rope runs through my hand during this pull, and that's what is supposed to happen. When I bring my hand forward again, I'll pitch the slack straight up, high in the air.

After the slack is pitched, my right hand will move to the horse's neck to tag him; or I might just pull back on the reins with my left hand—pull back to the saddle horn to signal a stop, then release the reins. I'll either tag and signal with the reins, or just signal with the reins, depending on the type of stop I want. Tagging a horse, placing my right hand on his neck about six inches from his ears, and pushing down—*not to the side*—will help a horse stop harder, and help him take the jerk of a heavy calf.

This cue helps the horse get his front feet into the ground a little better. The horse learns that he is about to stop when the slack is pitched, then he feels the reins pull back, and the tag on his neck...and he's into the stop. I won't tag a horse when I'm roping a light calf, usually, because I don't want a real strong stop that will jerk the calf down. The calf might not be getting to his feet by the time I'm there to flank him. And since he is a light calf, the horse really isn't going to need any extra help in absorbing the jerk.

But when I want to really help a horse stop, I'll tag and still be in the saddle—with my weight shifting to his hindquarters—when the jerk comes. My weight, shifted toward the cantle, will help him absorb the jerk of a heavy calf. As soon as the jerk has been absorbed, I'll continue my dismount, keeping my body

*Moving into the ideal position for a catch.*

*Just like running up to the dummy.*

71

*You can practice the dismount any time you get off your horse. Tag him, then dismount at a normal, quiet pace.*

*The left leg moves smoothly over the hindquarters.*

*And that's where you get off. Stay away from the horse's face.*

*1/ You get off the same way when things are moving a bit faster, during a roping run . . . .*

*2/*

*3/*

**I also dismount to the left a lot during practice. This helps the horse continue to stop straight.**

low, moving down and back over the hindquarters with my left leg. When I step out of the saddle, I want to get away cleanly, without pushing sideways off the horse. When my hand leaves his neck after the tag, I want to leave his head and forequarters alone at that point. A common mistake for beginners is to dismount while moving forward, next to the horse's face, and push off sideways. What this does is encourage the horse to move to his left; it teaches him a bad habit—he'll be out of the ground, jumping to the left, when he should be in the ground with his front feet, stopping straight with the calf.

I should also mention, at this point, that I dismount on the left side a lot during practice. I don't get off on the left side at rodeos, but I do during practice, because it helps the horse continue to stop straight.

The horse hasn't completely stopped when the roper dismounts; there is still plenty of forward motion, and this motion will help propel the roper down the rope. Remember to dismount low and back over the hindquarters; your feet should land fairly straight, parallel to the horse. Don't kick out of the right stirrup—just step out of it.

You can practice this dismount every time you get off your horse. If you get off to open a gate, for instance, step off at a normal pace, but get off low, over his back end, stepping away smoothly

with your toes pointing forward as each foot lands on the ground.

Back to the run...remember to run down the rope straight toward the calf. If the calf gets up and jumps sideways, change your angle so you're still moving directly to him with your left hand on the rope. And remember to run that left hand completely to the end of the rope, close to the calf; lift with that hand to keep his head up, block him off with your left leg as you reach across for the flank, and come under his belly and up with your right thigh, lifting with both hands, rolling him in the air for a good flat fall.

We've already discussed flanking and tying. The key points to remember are 1) proper body position over the calf, 2) pulling the top front foot into position for the tie as you step and string in one motion, and 3) gathering the hind feet and rolling your wrist to help position those feet in a perfect V that comes together in the middle of the calf's body. Tie close to the ground, rather than rolling the calf on his back with his feet high in the air. And when the tie is complete, throw your hands in the air as you stand.

Now mount your horse again and step him up so the rope is slack. In a rodeo, the field flagger will ride up to inspect the tie, and time for six seconds after the rope has been slackened. If the calf doesn't kick free in six seconds, the time

*This is the position to be in for an ideal catch. Notice also how the loop is curling upward into a figure-eight.*

*When tagging a horse for the stop, be sure to push straight down with your right hand.*

is recorded. At this point a couple of hands working the labor list at the rodeo will remove your loop and tie string. You can coil up your rope and put it across the saddle horn, and one of the assistants will hand you your piggin' string.

A practice session isn't all roping from a horse. You can practice roping a dummy, and you can practice just following a calf down the arena. When I was a kid, my dad had me follow a calf and swing an imaginary loop—I didn't have a rope in my hand, but I'd swing my arm and wrist and count all the times I could throw and catch: "Now, now," I'd count. My dad always told me not to throw until I was sure I could make a catch. And if I didn't do anything else right, I'd better at least be riding in a proper position—standing in the stirrups, raised up out of the saddle.

You can also practice just flanking and tying a calf, as discussed in those earlier chapters. I may flank and tie a calf 20 or 25 times; I want to wear myself out, get tired. I feel if I can rope and flank and tie without making mistakes when I'm tired, I can do it when I'm fresh, or tired, at a rodeo. I'm training my muscles and reactions. Everything becomes automatic and I don't have to really think. Whatever situation comes up—a calf that runs fast or slow, runs at an angle or doubles back; or maybe I don't make a clean neck catch; or maybe the calf kicks during the tie—whatever comes up, I've confronted it before in practice. And I'll react to it instinctively. That's what practice will do for you. It will help you physically and mentally if you try to get something good out of every run.

**I feel if I can rope and flank and tie without making mistakes when I'm tired, I can do it when I'm fresh.**

*A couple of shots of the jerk line at work. The pull is across my body, and the loops jerk free one at a time.*

75

*1/ Let's rope another one . . . .*

*2/ Grab the slack.*

*3/ Rip out the slack.*

*4/ Pitch it up.*

Your weight counterbalances the jerk on the saddle horn, and lessens the impact on the horse.

*5/ Tag the horse.*

*6/ Begin the dismount, but stay in the saddle long enough to help the horse absorb the jerk.*

There's still plenty of momentum at this point to propel the rider down the rope.

7/ Step off.

Keep your eyes on the calf and run straight for him.

*8/ Start down the rope.*

**Spring off your toes, like a sprinter in a race.**

*9/ The left arm goes over the rope.*

*10/ The left hand moves to the end of the rope while the left leg blocks the calf. The right hand is reaching for the flank.*

**Move under the calf and come straight up.**

*11/ Flank him.*

Don't step for-
ward or back-
ward. The lift is
straight up.

*12/ The lift . . . .*

*13/ Roll the calf in the air.*

*14/ Step and string at the same time.*

*15/ Throw the string to the side, in front of the hind legs. Then gather the legs and complete the tie.*

*16/ Signal for time.*

When the run is over, get back on the horse and step him up so the rope is slack. The un-tie man will remove the loop and pigging string.

# 8 PROBLEMS:
## CALVES, CATCHES
## & HORSES

## Problem Calves

If anything, I slow down a little when I'm dealing with a problem during a run. I don't want one mistake to lead to another.

Remember three things whenever you encounter a problem with a calf, whether the calf is kicking while you're trying to tie, or whether you've made a bad catch. Remember that you may still have a chance to win something, so don't give up; that your best bet whenever anything goes wrong is to automatically go into the two-handed tie; and that you can't make up for lost time by trying to hurry the tie. If anything, I slow down a little when I'm dealing with a problem during a run. I don't want one mistake to lead to another.

I won the 1982 calf roping championship on my last calf at the Finals, and I roped that calf by one hind foot. The time was 11.9 and I placed second in the ten-calf average. I was out of position when I threw—the calf had veered to the right—and rather than try to reposition my horse (Butch Stoneman's great rope horse Whit), I went on and threw my loop. Then the calf nearly ran through the loop before I was able to pull the slack. It was just one of those things you encounter periodically in rodeo; I made the best of it, and it worked. And you can do it, too, if you learn what to do in a bad situation, and practice.

Every pen of calves seems to have a certain percentage that invariably want to kick every time they're roped. You'll see a calf that has been flanked, and when the roper tries to gather the back legs to make his tie, the calf will kick out of his hand. The best way to try to avoid having a calf kick in the first place is to sit down on him and tie close to the ground, because a lot of calves will show more willingness to kick if they are

rolled on their backs with the feet high in the air during a tie. We discussed this earlier.

Assuming a roper is starting his tie close to the ground, and the calf still kicks, there is a sequence of moves to follow to counteract this. First, pause just a second; some calves will kick a couple of times, then lie still. If this fails, grab the calf's flank with your right hand; this will make him stop kicking. Then go ahead and try to gather the feet again for the tie. The third possibility is to gather just one hind foot—the bottom one—and get one wrap around that foot and a front foot, then gather in the other hind foot for another wrap, continuing with the two-handed tie. You can usually slip a wrap on, one at a time, by gathering just one foot at a time on a kicking or straining calf.

What do you do with a calf that's down when you get to him, and he doesn't want to get up? First thing is to maintain your grip on the rope with your left hand, reach under his head with your right hand, and pull it up toward your body. If he jumps up suddenly, your left hand is where it should be, and you can proceed with your right hand for flanking.

If the calf still doesn't get up, reach down with your right hand and try to get his feet out in front of him. If the horse is working properly, he'll usually pull the calf up. But if this fails, I'll continue to lift on the rope with my left hand while I grab his tail or flank with my right. If he's lying on his left side, with his feet away from me, I'll lift and push to get his feet under him. If his feet

90

*Calf roping is a fast-paced event. A lot of things can happen—for good or bad—in a short amount of time.*

**Photo by James Fain**

1/ If a calf isn't on his feet when you get to him, you'll have to help him up. Lift on the rope with your left hand. And if his feet are pointing toward you, reach across with the right hand to pull and lift.

2/ If that fails, move the right hand to his tail to pull and lift. The calf is getting to his feet, now.

*3/ Be ready to block him off with your left leg as he takes that first jump, and move the right hand back to the flank.*

*4/ Then go ahead and flank.*

*If a calf isn't up, and his feet are pointing away from you (top left), then pull on the rope with your left hand, and push and lift with your right hand as shown (top right).*

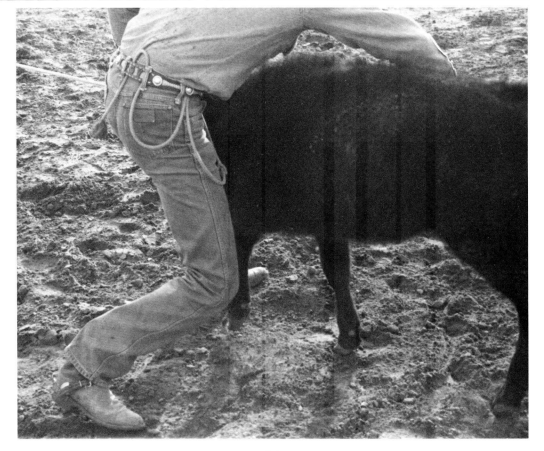

*Then block him off and flank him as he gets to his feet.*

*Here's a good way to flank a big, stout calf. Grab his nose and bend his head back.*

*And flank him like this.*

*1/ Here's a calf that decided to make a turn just as he was roped.*

*2/ The horse moved to the left a little, but the calf made a sharp turn to the right. So I threw my slack to the right, in an effort to get a clean fall, or to turn the calf around on his feet.*

3/ And it worked. Had I continued to throw the slack forward, rather than to the right, the calf probably would have taken a rolling fall and not been on his feet as I was getting to him.

are toward me, the procedure is simply reversed. I'll lift and *pull* his feet toward me and under him. Once he's up, he can be flanked or legged down for a legal fall and normal tie.

## Problem Catches

Say you rope a calf by one hind foot. You're usually on the right side because you've dismounted on the right. Usually the calf is going to jump up and be standing up, facing away from you, with that rope on one hind leg while your horse is backing up. So reach down with your right hand to grab his right front leg, grab his flank with your left hand, and use this method to leg him down on his side. Step across with your left foot, and place the string on the bottom front foot. Drop your right knee to the ground, between his back legs, then gather the bottom foot that hasn't been roped, and bring it up to the front foot for one wrap. Then place the other front foot, get another wrap around the three feet,

and complete the tie.

If a calf has been roped by both hind feet, you're faced with a little more of a problem—you've got to remove the loop before you can tie. The horse will be back on the rope, if he's working properly, so leg the calf down, then quickly pull the calf toward the horse—just far enough to put some slack in the rope—and slip off the loop. *Keep your hands on the calf;* don't let him get away. Go ahead and tie.

If a calf is caught around the belly, leg him down. If he's facing away from you, turn him around, block him off, and leg him down. Then just make sure you pull the top front foot far enough back so your tie won't get tangled in the catch rope. Complete the tie as you would normally, using the two-handed method.

If you catch a front foot, or the head and a front foot, flank the calf and make the tie, stringing whichever front foot isn't in the loop. Again, use the two-handed tie.

Remember, also, that any time you ac-

**The only time your knee should be on the ground while making a tie is when you've caught the calf by a hind foot.**

1/ If a calf is caught by a hind foot, go ahead and string the top front foot to start with.

2/ Then grab the free hind foot.

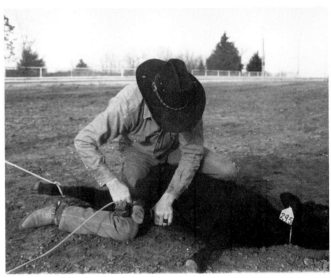

3/ Pull it forward and drop your right knee to the ground to help hold the foot.

4/ Put a wrap on the two feet you have.

5/ Then grab the other front foot.

6/ And complete the tie . . . .

7/

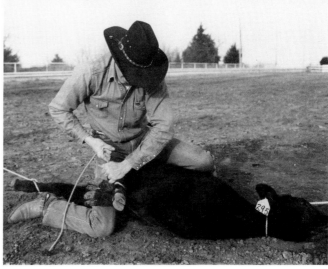

8/

9/

10/

11/

12/

*1/ If a calf is caught by the head and one front leg, grab whichever foot is free to begin the tie.*

*2/ String the foot.*

*3/ And complete the tie . . . .*

*4/ Remember to use the two-handed tie.*

*1/ If you accidentally string your hand along with the foot, just go ahead and gather the hind feet.*

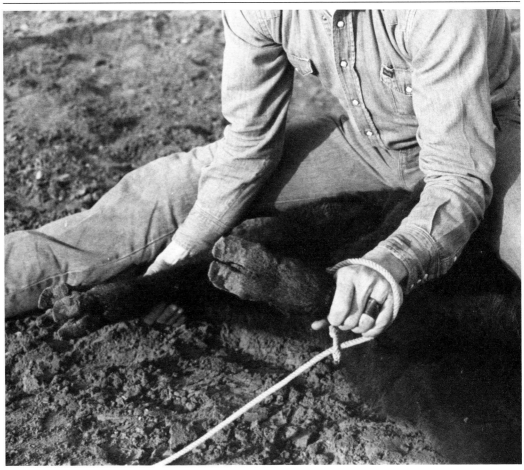

*2/ Put one wrap on all three feet.*

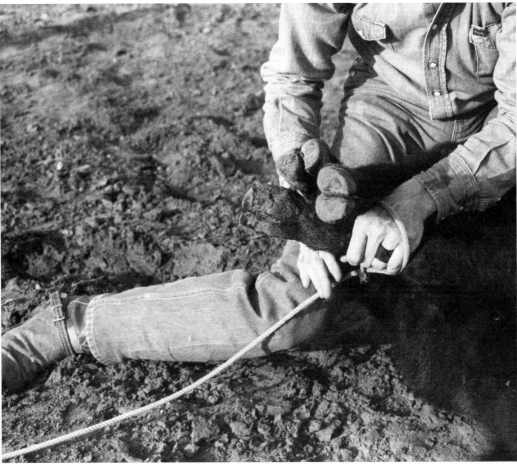

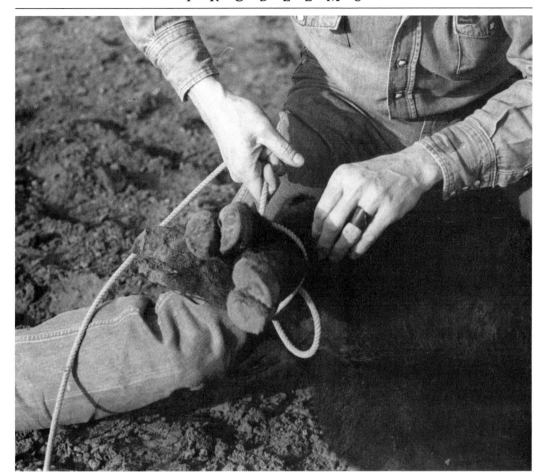

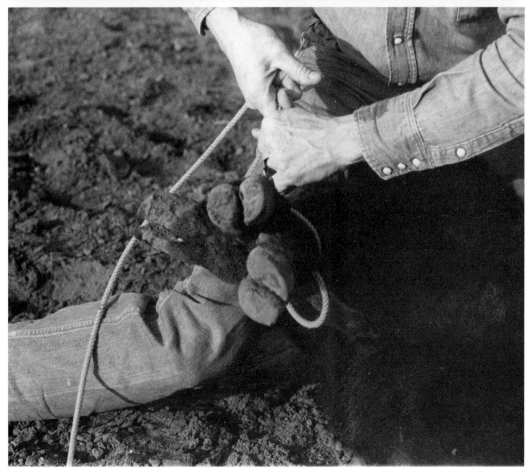

*3/ And slip your hand out of the loop as you complete the first wrap.*

*If you string a dew claw, use the two-handed method for a more secure tie.*

*4/ Then proceed with the two-handed tie.*

**If a horse is bad in the box, he needs time to readjust his thinking.**

*Spend plenty of time in the box, letting the horse relax.*

cidentally place the piggin' string around your hand while holding the front foot, to go on and take one wrap around the legs, remove your hand, and continue with the two-handed tie. If you accidentally string a dew claw, react to it automatically by going into the more secure two-handed tie. This will prevent the

string from slipping during the tie.

## Problem Horses

Well, so much for problems on the far end of the rope. Let's talk about some common problems at the other end, with the horse. The most common problems

hampions

1/ An alleyway can be used to help correct problems.

2/ If a horse is setting up—stopping before you cue him, while you rope—you can rope a calf . . . .

3/ Then kick the horse back into a lope after he tries to stop.

4/ Trail the calf, then cue the horse for a stop when you want to stop—not when he wants to.

that arise include bad behavior in the box, ducking off to the left or not getting into the ground properly for a good stop, and not working the rope while the calf is being flanked and tied.

If a horse is bad in the box—doesn't want to go in the box, or once he is in, tries to rear or turn or charge out before the roper wants him to—it's a sign the horse needs time to readjust his thinking. If he knows every time he is in the box that he'll have to run out just as fast and hard as he can until he's made to stop just as fast and hard as he can, he won't have anything to look forward to. And he'll start acting up.

But if the horse learns that he won't have to do that every single time he's in there, and that sometimes he'll just stand and relax awhile, then walk out, he'll settle down. So you teach this by spending a lot of time just standing in the box,

maybe getting off and loosening the cinches, letting him relax. And you score some calves on him—after roping a few calves, you turn one out and hold the horse in; you don't rope. Do this occasionally throughout the roping session, and the horse will become more relaxed and responsive. He'll leave the box when you want him to, not when he wants to, trying to anticipate or avoid the stress of a run.

If a horse isn't stopping properly when you rope a calf, you need to figure out why. Is he sore somewhere? A saddle that doesn't fit properly can make a horse sore-backed, and he won't want to stop hard when you rope a calf. Does he throw his head up and move to the left when you're getting off on the right while roping? A horse should stop straight with the calf whether the roper dismounts from the right or left; if he's

*I prefer to use ordinary shoes on my horses.*

moving away from the roper during a stop and dismount, it often means the roper isn't getting out of the saddle properly. He's probably pushing away from the horse, actually teaching the horse to move sideways, rather than dismounting low over the hindquarters, and moving straight down to the ground. Maybe the horse needs to have some roping off both sides, left and right. Maybe he needs a little tighter, or a little more severe, tie-down. If that's the case, make sure that he can get away from the discomfort if his head is positioned properly. You want him to be able to get away from any pain he feels as soon as he moves his head back down to a normal head position. The whole reason for wanting his head down, rather than high in the air, is so his front feet will stay in the ground for a good stop. Another possible cure that might be used in conjunction with a readjusted tie-down would be a change in bits. Maybe he needs a stronger bit. If he's in a snaffle, maybe a bit with a port in it would work better. Or maybe his bit needs longer shanks. Or, if he's light-mouthed, maybe he needs a less-severe bit.

The bottom line is this: If a horse is having trouble staying in the ground, it's best to experiment with his head gear, rather than to do something with his feet, like putting corks on his shoes. With corks, a horse's front feet will be sucked into the ground during a stop, but they'll make him break over. Once his feet are in the ground as far as they can go during a stop, he'll have to take them out of the ground again until his forward motion has ended. The only time I'd recommend doing something different to a horse's shoes is if his hind feet are sliding too far forward, interfering with his front feet during a stop. In that case, a trailer on the outside of each hind shoe will spread his back legs just enough so those feet don't slide into the front feet.

If the horse isn't working the rope properly—isn't backing up a step or two, keeping the rope tight while you're flanking and tying the calf—you might try getting a stronger pull on the jerk line. Maybe the jerk line should be adjusted for a pull across your body, with the loops tucked under your belt on the right side. Or maybe you need to get a stronger pull by tightening your belt a notch.

Remember, too, that too much work on a jerk line will gradually make the horse's mouth hard. You can practice with a jerk line to the point where you and your horse know what it is and what it will do. And you can help keep him tuned up with it so he works the rope good. And you use it, usually, in competition. But most of the practicing should be done without it; that just saves his mouth.

Every good rope horse does need to be tuned up periodically. What that amounts to is, during a practice session, you're practicing for the horse, not yourself. You might spend a week doing some outside riding—just riding him, giving him a change of scenery, something other than roping. But each day you might rope just three or four calves on him, concentrating on doing everything correctly. You work on rating calves, on maintaining proper position behind; and when you rope, you want to help your horse stop straight—rope a couple calves off both sides. And help the horse stop by tagging him and staying in the saddle just a bit longer to make sure he stays in the ground. This is also a good time to be using a jerk line on the horse. The whole idea is to have a series of short, relaxing practices, concentrating on doing everything correctly, and not so much on speed.

I don't try to keep my horses "topped out" all the time. I want them to be at their best at the best rodeos or ropings. The better the horse is, the easier it is to win.

I don't try to keep my horses "topped out" all the time. I want them to be at their best at the best rodeos and ropings.

*If a horse starts turning to the left while stopping, roping several calves in a row and dismounting on the left side will help straighten him out.*

*1/ Here's a good run in progress.*

*2/ The slack is pitched.*

*3/ The horse is being tagged for the stop.*

*4/ I step off.*

*5/ And start down the rope.*

*6/ My left arm goes over the rope.*

7/ And it looks like
the calf isn't going to
get up.

8/ So I block him off
and reach.

9/ Lifting with my left
hand; pushing and
lifting with my right.

**10/** *The calf is up.*

11/ *And I can flank him.*

12/ *I grab the top front leg.*

13/ *And step and string . . . .*

14/ *. . . at the same time.*

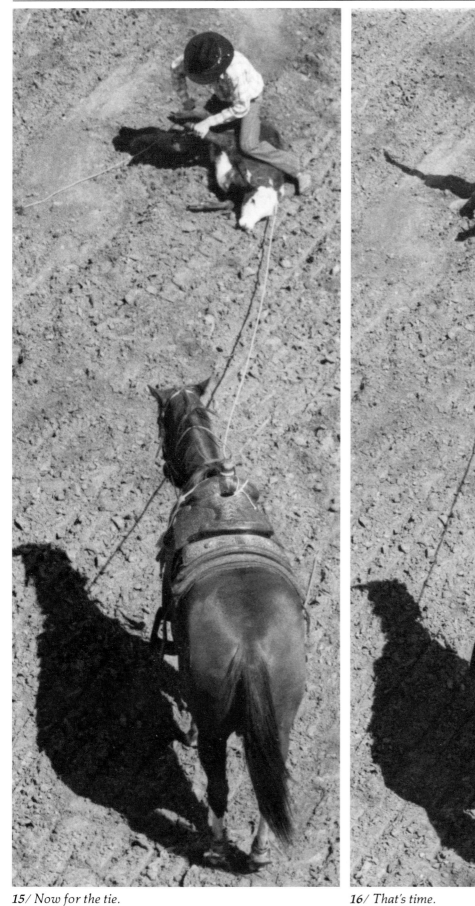

*15/* Now for the tie.

*16/* That's time.

# 9  ROPE HORSE TRAINING

*Roy Cooper's dad tells what it takes to train a horse for roping.*

**I believe there is no such thing as quick horse training. The only answer is a lot of patience and a lot of riding.**

Most everything I learned about training, I learned from the old-time horse trainers. When I was growing up, you just didn't go out and buy a high-priced horse, you tried to make your own rope horse. Nearly everyone did this, and there were a lot of good trainers around.

It takes a lot of time and patience to turn out a good horse and keep him working. And I guess the older you get, the more patience you acquire. A friend, James Kenney, once said, "When you're old enough to keep a horse working, you're too old to win." That may be true. Of course a person who continues to train horses will continue to gain knowledge through the years, so that's a factor. Aside from that, I don't think there is any substitute for *riding*. I'll explain the type of riding I do momentarily.

I like a stout horse, 1,125 to 1,250 pounds, and around 15 hands—big enough not to get pulled off balance by the calf, or by the roper when he steps off. I like an athletic horse with kind of a short neck, a horse that is intelligent and quick, has a good disposition, and works quietly. Some horses really pound the ground when they run, and this can make a difference when the roping is being done over a long score line, like the 30-foot score at Cheyenne. If a calf hears the horse coming from a long way off, he'll run harder and it will take longer to catch him.

An athletic horse should be able to do anything, whether you make a rope horse out of him, or use him for barrel racing, team roping, bulldogging, or pleasure. And you can't go against good breeding—in other words, if you select a young horse from a line of horses that have proven themselves in competition, then that horse will probably work. If you go against good breeding, you're taking a greater chance of ending up with a horse that may not work the way you want him to. However, I don't believe the really top horses were simply born to greatness—their trainers made them great.

I really break a horse good before I start him on roping. I want the horse to respond well to the bit, and have a good stop. And I don't want a "chargey" horse—I'd rather have to push a horse a little than to hold him back all the time. I also do a lot of pasture work while I'm breaking a horse—I'll make a cow horse out of him. I've never wanted a rope horse that I couldn't take out of the arena to work or rope cattle in the open.

When I'm starting a horse on roping, I do a lot of riding to get him tired before I even begin in the arena. And I do a lot of ground work to get him used to working a rope. I'll use a jerk line at times to keep him back on the rope. For example, I'll lope down the arena, throw the rope on the ground in front of him, stop and step off—on the left side, rather than the right (that will come much later). I'll go down the rope a ways while the jerk line takes over, then I'll pick up the rope and

114

*A horse has got to learn to work a rope properly, to maintain an even amount of pressure on the calf. This helps the roper flank and tie. But don't let the horse "over-work" the rope (continue backing)—that's a hindrance to the roper, because it makes the calf struggle and kick.*

face him. I'll shake the rope, if necessary, to get him back.

I also teach a horse his cue for stopping during these early sessions. I don't like to yank on his mouth, but I will take hold of him. I want him to know he should be prepared to stop when I throw the rope, and to go into the stop as soon as I pull back on the reins and tag him.

If a horse is having problems standing still, maintaining a tight rope, I'll rope a dummy, then go sit on the dummy, watch the horse and make him stand tight against the rope. And I'll sit there and work with him like this for perhaps an hour.

During this phase of training, I'll also work on scoring and rating cattle. I'll have a pen of calves, and have the horse in the box like we're ready to rope. I want the horse to be attentive, to watch the calf in the chute; and I'll have someone rattle the chute gate, so the horse gets used to the noise. Then the calf will be turned out and I'll just hold the horse in the box. Then I might leave the box on

*Having the right kind of calves is an important part of rope horse training. I never use real hard-running calves, or calves that are roped-out (learned some erratic tricks that make it harder to trail them) on a young horse.*

*The horse needs to learn how to trail cattle, and how to rate them.*

ing the rope, I'll just sit on the calf, shake the rope back to the horse, and get him to back up. Once he's working properly, I'll go ahead and tie.

Each training session will last several hours, but I probably won't rope more than four or five calves in any one session. I may rope two or three in a row, and then let the horse rest and think about it for awhile. I might just let the horse stand, with the cinch loosened, or I might ride around the arena or out in pasture for awhile. Then I'll come back later and rope a couple more on him. I'll also continue to use him for general cow work, gathering or checking cattle. And I'll drag logs on him, too, so he won't be afraid of the rope, no matter what it is tied to, whether it is in front of him or behind.

As for head gear, one thing I like to use during training is a nose chain. The chain has a loop in it; the rope runs through the loop, then under the neck rope, and attaches to the saddle horn. This chain keeps the horse's head straight with the calf, after it has been roped. I also usually start roping with a steel tie-down that is adjusted so it's pretty snug. This takes the charge out of a horse, makes him run with his head down, and affords greater control over him. As for bits, every horse is an individual, so I just keep changing bits until I find one that seems to best suit that particular horse.

I don't like to rope in an alley, although a narrow alley can be helpful if a horse develops a real problem trailing calves and rating them. The confinement of an alley can help correct a problem, but I don't like to start there. I would rather the horse learn to watch cattle and trail them in a big arena. Arena training takes longer, but builds a better foundation in the horse, in my opinion.

I believe there is no such thing as quick horse training. The only answer is a lot of patience and a lot of riding—really getting the horse broke. Don't expect too much of a horse too early in his training. Don't do a lot of whipping on him, correcting mistakes. Good common sense and hard work with patience will produce more top horses than anything I know.

I've got to add a note to beginning ropers at this point, and to parents of

the next couple calves, then score one, then trail several more calves down through the arena. We'll work on maintaining position, on rating; and it's important during these early stages to use a pen of slow calves. I never run worn-out calves or hard-running calves on a young horse. I believe many horses are ruined—more than anything else during the early days of their careers—by using the wrong type of calves.

The next step is to set up a barrier rope, so the horse gets accustomed to the rope snapping back, simulating rodeo conditions. And I'll start breakaway roping on him, using a rope with a breakaway honda. I'll spend six months on a horse with ground work and breakaway roping before I ever tie a calf. When I rope a calf and the rope breaks free, I'll still step off and continue to pick up the rope so the horse can work it.

When the horse has reached the point where he is scoring good, rating good, stops and gets back on the rope, then I'll start tying. The calves will still be slow, and I won't take a bad throw. I'll trail a calf quite a ways and make sure the horse is in perfect position to stop—directly behind the calf. And I'll continue to step off on the left, and go down the rope (staying on the left side) to help the horse stay straight with the calf. If I'm tying a calf and see the horse not work-children who want to rope. Don't try to train your own horse. There are still parents who think, "Well, I'll buy a young horse for my kid, and the two of them can learn together." That's a big mistake. Get an old solid horse that doesn't make mistakes, so all the novice roper has to think about is learning to rope. It's also best to get a small horse for a youngster, rather than a big horse. A kid can see the calf better on a small horse, and he'll swing a better loop.

And I think it's better to be under-mounted than over-mounted. If you've got a horse you have to push a little, that will force you to hustle more, and to think. I once had a horse that couldn't run very fast, and I knew I had to get out of that barrier perfectly, or I'd get outrun. Well, I learned how to get out.

*—Tuffy Dale Cooper*

*If a horse is having problems standing still, maintaining a tight rope, you can rope a dummy, then go sit on the dummy, watch the horse and make him stand tight against the rope.*

*Don't expect too much of a horse too early in his training.*

117

# 10 RODEOING & WINNING

**I try to go as fast as I can on every run without making a mistake.**

Rodeo has become a big mental game in many respects. Anyone who has followed the sport knows this, because a lot of champions have talked for years about the importance of having "a good attitude." What it boils down to, I think, is knowing yourself, knowing what you can do, and rising above all the little adversities that anyone faces rodeoing day to day.

If my horse is working and I'm roping good, that's enough for me, mentally. If my horse isn't working or I'm not roping as good as I think I should, that will hurt me mentally, but I've learned to overcome those things. You hear about being in a hot streak, or a cold streak, and how that affects cowboys mentally. There is something to that. When you're winning, it seems so easy. When you're not winning, rodeo is work.

One thing I believe—you can get out of a cold streak as fast as you got into it. There are times when a contestant feels he is working so hard to win, and time after time something goes wrong: he breaks the barrier, he draws bad, he gets out of the box late. You can't get discouraged; you can't make up for lost time by hurrying faster than you should and increasing the chance of making a mistake. Stick to the basics, analyze any mistakes, and work to correct problems. If you're roping good, but not winning, tell yourself you'll get out of this cold streak

as fast as you got into it, and be ready to win when you draw a good calf. Most everyone can become a good roper. Everybody can't be a world champion, but an average roper can beat a world champion if he is prepared to do everything right when he draws a good calf.

There are other aspects to this mental game. I was pumped up and ready to rope at Calgary in 1982, the year I won a $50,000 bonus there. And the next day I was roping for $600 at Spanish Fork, Utah, competing against a lot of the same ropers who were at Calgary. It was hard for me to prepare myself mentally to rope. I felt a tendency to want to just lay back after the Calgary win, but I knew I had to fight that. Anyone who puts up his money to compete at a rodeo, big or little, had better be ready to give it all he has, or he might as well have not entered. So, that's mental, too.

I try to go as fast as I can on every run without taking a chance on making a mistake. I don't want to get out of control, where my mind is moving faster than my hands. All I think about is not beating myself. And when I'm roping good and my horse is working good, all I really have to concentrate on is scoring well. I'll be on a roll, and it's like nothing can go wrong. I'll be rodeoing hard and winning, and it's great. Then suddenly, after maybe several weeks of this, I'll be worn out; I'll stop winning.

That's when I need to back off. Whether it's mental or physical or both, I know myself, and I know when I need a break. I'll go home for a day or two, be with my family, and do whatever I feel I need to do. Maybe I'll get completely away from roping for a day, not even think about it. Maybe I'll practice. I remember one summer, roping with Arnold Felts, I got tired and wasn't winning. And I said, "Man, if I could just have two days of practice, it would help me." He said, "No, it won't help you. You've practiced all your life." He was right in a way, but I kept rodeoing and not winning, and finally, after I went home and just practiced for a couple days, and sat around the house for a day or two, I went back to rodeoing…and I killed 'em. Was that something mental? Probably. All I know is, it works for me.

Some other things I do that help me mentally when I'm on the road: I like to have as many travel and other arrangements worked out ahead of time, before I've even left; if I'm not taking my own horse, I want to have a horse lined up to ride before I get there; even if I'm traveling with several other guys, I like to get my own motel room, just to have some time to myself. You're surrounded by people at a rodeo; it helps me to get away from that a little bit when I stop to rest.

Something else I learned about myself—I can get burned out trying to get to more rodeos than I should. I remember rodeoing with Ernie Taylor the first year I was in the PRCA. We went to five rodeos one day. We started at 8 a.m. slack in Ada, Okla., and I wound up winning that rodeo. Then I roped at Burlington in eastern Colorado at 2 p.m., then at Evergreen in the mountains west of Denver at 4:30. We flew back to Dodge City, Kan., for the rodeo at 8,

*Roy Cooper, at Prescott, Ariz., 1984.*
**Photo by James Fain**

*At Tucson, 1984.*
**Photo by James Fain**

**There are some real nuts and bolts to winning— things to do, adjustments to make from one rodeo to the next.**

then went to Henderson north of Denver for slack roping late that night. I didn't place at any of those other four rodeos that day. I believe I was thinking more about the travel connections than I was about roping. I was rolling too fast.

When you're rodeoing, you've got to learn to relax and sleep whenever the opportunity is there. You might be roping in late-night slack one day, and early-morning slack the next, so the hours vary. I used to wake up at 7:30 if I had slack at 8 a.m. I'd just have time to get to the arena, pay my fees, see what calf I drew, and then rope. I'd still be half asleep when I nodded my head to rope. Now I'll get up at 6 a.m., and I'll go

ahead and feed my horse and give him time to digest his food. He'll be ready to rope at 8 and I'll be wide awake—I'll be ready, too. I don't like to have the horse work on a real full stomach, though, and I feel the same about myself. Your hours do get messed up. When I'm through roping late at night, that's when I'll have breakfast. Eating properly is a challenge for anyone who rodeos, because we have a tendency to eat a lot of fast foods. A contestant will do better mentally and physically if he trains himself to stop and eat a balanced meal at least once a day.

There are some real nuts and bolts to winning—things to do, adjustments to make from one rodeo to the next. First

I'll see what calf I've drawn. Then I'll see what's winning and what's placing. I'll analyze the times. I'll look at that calf, maybe find out what has been done on him before, and see what I think I can tie him in. I'll check out the score line. If I've got a good calf, I know I've got to score good. The surest way to mess up a good calf is to break the barrier or get out late. If you can get out good on a good calf—be within six or 12 inches of the barrier rope when it trips—you're usually going to win. I feel that way.

If I've got a good calf, I might try to see his shoulder move to the barrier pin on the side of the chute, then signal my horse to start. And I'd probably quarter my horse in the box—the horse will have to take one extra step, but that will allow just a little bit more room. I don't want to be late, but I sure don't want to break the barrier.

If I'm up in the first section of roping, I'll just plan to go as fast as I can without making a mistake. The advantage of being up later in the rodeo, or at the end, is that you know what you have to beat. Sometimes I'll arrive and find they've tied the heck out of those calves, and I've drawn a sorry calf. In that case, I won't

be thinking about winning first, but I'll do all I can to place. Maybe I'd be lucky to place at all, but I won't give up mentally before I've even roped.

At a rodeo that has fresh calves—calves that have never been roped—I'd probably use a little tighter tie-down on my horse, tuck his head just a little more than usual, because a fresh calf usually won't run very fast when he leaves the chute, and I want plenty of control on the horse. I'll have to kick the horse to the calf; and the horse will sure rate the calf with a slightly tighter tie-down. Something else I'll be sure to do on a fresh calf is tie his feet very close to the ground, trying to ease his feet together for the tie. Fresh calves will usually kick more than calves that have already been roped several times.

If I'm roping over a long score line—say at Cheyenne where it's 30 feet—I'll probably loosen the tie-down more than usual so the horse can run more freely. At least I'll be sure to do this for the second go-round; Cheyenne uses fresh calves, so they leave the chute slowly the first time, quickly the second time. I might even take the bit off my horse and use a hackamore bit, but that just goes

*Odessa, Tex., 1981.*
**Photo by James Fain**

back to knowing your horse and what equipment works on him.

The same thing applies to jerk lines. If I'm roping a fairly small, light calf, I don't want a real hard stop for him. If that calf gets jerked down hard, he might be slow getting to his feet, and that will cost me time if I have to help him up before I flank him. So if I use a jerk line, I'll want it tucked two or three times under my belt on the left side for a light pull. But if I've got a big, stout calf, I may rig up the jerk line for an across-the-body pull on my right; and I might even tighten my belt a notch so that jerk line really makes the horse scramble to get back on the rope.

Again, it's a matter of knowing your horse, knowing how he works. Some horses stop mostly with their front end,

others really get their hindquarters under them and stop that way. Some have a quick suck-back on the rope, others stop and hesitate, then back up a couple steps. Some horses will pull a calf at a slight angle towards you, which is what you want; others will pull at a slight angle away from you as you run down the rope.

After people learn to rope pretty well, they try to "control their go-rounds." They figure out what kind of calf they think they have drawn, and make what preparations they can ahead of time. And after they've nodded for the calf and the run is in progress, they react to how the calf is running. You can help control your go's to some extent by the way in which you handle your slack.

I guess anyone who has watched me

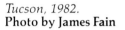

*Tucson, 1982.*
**Photo by James Fain**

rope through the years has seen me handle my slack in a variety of ways. I've held it and pitched it while I was running to the calf, I've thrown it to the right, to the left. I was trying to do different things with different calves. Say I've got a slower calf: I run up on him, my momentum is up and I've got a lot of rope in my hand, I might throw it and step off with the slack in my hand. People think I'm letting the calf pull me, but I'm not, really.

I'm just holding the rope while I step off; then I'll drop it. To tell the truth, I don't drop or pitch the slack from the ground much any more, at least not the way I used to, because I think there is more risk of getting your hand caught in the rope, and I know what that's like literally from firsthand experience. But I've done that on light or slow calves for two reasons: 1) I was trying to stop them without jerking them down—remember, pitching slack from the saddle is the first signal the horse gets for a hard stop. And 2) it's faster than staying in the saddle, helping the horse prepare for the jerk.

Anyway, that's why I've done it, but I can't recommend this procedure to anyone else, because it does have its pitfalls. And while a guy can get away with it occasionally on light calves, a horse will stop working if the roper makes a habit of this, because it does cheat the horse. The horse doesn't get a good signal to prepare for the jerk. I started roping like that in the amateurs around my old home country because the calves we roped were all light, and you really didn't need a horse to work a rope. Once I got in the PRCA, where the calves are heavier, I learned to actually slow down a bit in order to win.

Now, if a calf is roped and he suddenly veers to your right, pitching the slack to the right will probably get a cleaner fall. Pitching the slack straight up or to the left will most likely result in a rolling fall, and the calf probably won't be getting to his feet when you're ready to flank.

If a calf ducks to the left, you really can't pitch the slack very far to the left because your horse's head is in the way. Just pitch it straight up or up and slightly to the left—you'll usually get a clean fall or get the calf hopped around on his feet without the fall. In fact, pitching the

slack high and slightly to the left or right on a straight-running calf will usually bring him around on his feet, or produce a clean fall, depending on the stop you get. Shooting the slack straight up high will bring a calf straight back for a clean fall, too. What you want to avoid is pitching your slack straight and low, letting it roll over his back—that's what can injure a calf.

On a horse that has a hair-trigger stop, and really sucks back on that rope, you're going to be limited with what you can do with your slack. You certainly won't be able to hold it. The best bet is to stick with the basics—pitch the slack straight up, or straight up and to the left or right slightly. And after all, that is the perfect way to rope. Ninety percent of the time, it will work, regardless of what the calf does.

I do think it's important to rip that slack out as fast as you can during a normal run. I use rawhide burners, rather than leather burners, because the rawhide is faster. You can pull the slack easier and therefore faster with the rawhide burners. You also wear out a rope faster with this type of burner. I can wear out a rope in a day's practice if I rope, say, 50 calves. The rope will start breaking down; you'll see a frayed spot. Naturally, I won't use a rope like that at a rodeo and take a chance on it breaking.

I can rope effectively with a variety of ropes, but one thing I don't like to change very often is my piggin' string. Most ropers feel the same way. Once I have a string I feel comfortable with, that seems easiest to handle and tie, I like to hang on to it. I sure don't want to be at a rodeo with a string I'm not used to.

**I can rope effectively with a variety of ropes, but one thing I don't like to change very often is my piggin' string.**

*Salt Lake City, 1977.*
**Photo by James Fain**

*Tucson, 1980.*
**Photo by James Fain**

This isn't just a mental hang-up, not when we're dealing in fractions of seconds.

Roping competition has become tougher in recent years. Jerk lines and roping schools have contributed to this. There's also a general willingness to take chances. A guy has to take a chance to win sometimes, but it's a very fine line. You've got to stick with the basics, but still gamble now and then. You react. Do you throw now, or take another swing or two and get into better position? If you throw now and catch, it might mean the difference between placing or not placing, or winning first and just placing. Of course if you miss, well, there's always another rodeo.

124

*National Finals Rodeo, 1983.*

**Photo by James Fain**

# 11 PROFILE:
# ROY COOPER
## *"I'll always rope."*

*Roy, age 3, on a horse named Big Track.*

ROY COOPER remembers arriving home from school, stepping off the bus, and seeing the horses saddled in the arena, ready for roping. "Dad wanted me to rope," he says. "He wanted to teach me, and I wanted to learn. He was a good teacher, and I was a good student. We roped every day after school; and summers he would roll us kids out of bed at 6 a.m., so we could help with whatever work had to be done around the ranch that day. He liked to get an early start so we could finish up in the afternoon and have plenty of time for roping."

Tuffy Dale and Betty Rose Cooper raised three children on their ranch in eastern New Mexico near Monument, 30 miles from Hobbs. And all three—Betty Gayle, Roy and Clay—grew up learning to ride and rope. Roy went on to rope his way into the record books, while Betty Gayle became an all-around and calf roping champion herself in women's rodeo. And now younger brother Clay is proving to be a capable hand in PRCA calf roping. Of course, cousin Jimmie Cooper, whose family also ranches in the area, was all-around champ in 1981. Roping was, and still is, a way of life for the Coopers.

Such lifestyles are fairly common in rodeo—particularly roping circles. And the eastern New Mexico area alone can boast of a long line of famous ropers before Roy came along. Past champions like Jake McClure, Richard Merchant, Troy Fort, Sonny Davis, and Olin Young began their roping careers in the open arid rangeland.

Roy wanted to be a cowboy all along.

Betty Rose remembers her scarf collection disappeared the summer Roy was five years old. Roy had been riding a Welsh pony around the ranch, following a hired man who was doctoring cattle for screwworms and pinkeye—and he was using Mom's scarfs as "wild rags" to tie around his neck.

By the time Roy was ten, he was riding a little Quarter Horse named Scooter, who had been trained for calf roping: "He'd follow a calf through a keyhole," Tuffy says. "He scored good," adds Roy. "And he had a pretty good stop and would back up a step or two."

Roy learned to catch calves with his rope unattached to the saddle horn; he would catch and let go of the rope. It was his decision to start tying his rope to the saddle, and the first time he tried it (without Dad's knowledge), he discovered the importance of a back cinch—because he didn't have one on his saddle. Roy made a dandy catch and was subsequently launched out of the saddle when it tipped forward as the calf hit the end of the rope.

"I always dreamed about the kids growing up to be good ropers," Tuffy says. "But I was afraid Roy might not be big enough for the event. He didn't really start growing until he was nearly out of high school." Roy also had to contend with an asthma condition, which still flares up occasionally.

But those were minor obstacles in the path of a youngster who wanted to excel in roping and other sports. Roy played on a youth football team, and when the asthma bothered him, he would tape a spray bottle of decongestant to his hand,

"I was afraid Roy might not be big enough for the event. He didn't really start growing until he was nearly out of high school."

*Three-year-old Roy in 1958. He wanted to be a cowboy all along.*

*Betty Gayle and Roy on Frosty, at the Cooper Ranch, 1956.*

*On Big Track, again, 1959.*

*Scooter—Roy's first calf roping horse: "A real dandy."*

for use between plays. Despite his size, he played successfully for the Heizer Junior High School Hornets' basketball team; the coach said Roy was quick with his hands.

"I remember the day I got off the bus carrying my new basketball uniform. Dad was waiting down at the arena, like always, but I just had to try on that uniform. And then I thought I'd just shoot a few baskets, to see how it felt."

Tuffy watched Roy playing basketball at the house while he stood waiting with horses, ready for the usual afternoon roping session. The normal routine was for Roy to practice school sports in the morning, before class, and to practice

*Roy, 8, and brother Clay, 4, during a roping at Monument.*

roping after school. But one basket led to another, and another, and Roy was suddenly Wilt Chamberlain making the game-winning basket. He was ready to quit when he looked out at the arena and saw Dad leading the horses through a gate to "the big pasture."

"Any time you turned a horse into 'the big pasture,' it meant you weren't figuring on using that horse again in the near future. That just killed me. I felt bad, but I knew Dad felt bad, too. He said if I wasn't interested in roping any longer, we wouldn't rope. Well, I guess about a week went by, and one day I got off the bus and saw those horses saddled up in the arena. I don't know which of us was happier to be roping again. I know we both were miserable that week we didn't rope."

The practice sessions would last till dark, and it was always Roy who made certain all the calves were roped. "The

*Roy and Beaver.*

*At 14, Roy was playing basketball for the Heizer Hornets.*

**"I get a lot of credit for training Roy," Tuffy says. "But it was their mom who hauled the kids to most of those rodeos."**

rest of us would be ready to quit roping, but if there were calves left in the pen, Roy couldn't stand to just turn them out. He had to rope them," Tuffy says. "When we were through roping, we would tie maybe 50 calves; just practice tying them before we went to the house for supper. But that still wouldn't be enough for Roy. He'd go outside afterwards and practice tying a dummy calf under the yard light. I made him a crude little dummy out of a square block of wood a couple feet long. There were three rubber hoses attached to it, and each hose had a wad of tape on the end—those were the legs and feet. He could gather the legs and practice his tie. And that's where he really learned his speed—by tying that dummy."

When the weather was cold, Roy practiced tying with gloves on his hands.

Tuffy helped Roy develop his tie, taking what he thought was the best he had seen in other ropers. "I liked the way Olin Young would string a calf and take that first wrap; I liked the way he handled kicking calves by tying low to the ground. And it always seemed to me Don McLaughlin would put on the fastest second wrap. For the hooey and getting away from the calf real quick, it was Ronnye Sewalt." He coached Roy on leaving the box, patterning Troy Fort's start: "I liked the way Troy got his rope up and was in position to catch real quick."

"He coached me till I was probably 16," says Roy. "While I was roping, he was teaching me, telling me what to do: 'Get your arm up…get your slack right …don't throw until you know you can catch this calf.' Or he might say, 'If you don't do anything else this run, stand up in those stirrups. I don't care if you catch or miss, but stand up in those stirrups.'

"He'd have me rope little Holstein calves, and get my confidence up. I'd make a lot of fast runs, and really be hustling. Then he would bring in a bunch of wild calves, right off the cows, and I'd just get knocked down and discouraged.

"I remember one time," Roy smiles. "I was trying to leg one down for so long, and not getting him on the ground, that Dad walked out there and threatened to spank me with a piggin' string if I didn't get that calf legged down. The second

time he walked out there I got the calf down. I was so little trying to get those calves down…I'd get tired. But he wouldn't let me quit. He taught me to never quit once I started something."

The Cooper kids joined the American Junior Rodeo Association, based in Texas. The AJRA is undoubtedly the most competitive of the youth rodeo organizations. The youngsters compete for cash, not ribbons. No one worries about the question of amateur sports status because the youngsters are usually serious about striving for a pro career in rodeo anyway. The Coopers would compete in 40 to 50 AJRA rodeos a year. Roy was rodeoing by the time he was 10 years old.

"I get a lot of credit for training Roy," Tuffy says. "But it was their mom who hauled the kids to most of those rodeos. And she'd watch the calves and talk to the kids. She helped them at the rodeos."

When he was 12, Roy went to 50 junior rodeos and never missed a calf in the breakaway roping. He also entered tie-down roping, and his best time that year was 15 seconds. When he was 15 years old, he was tying calves in nine seconds.

Good horses are also an important element for success in roping, and Tuffy kept the kids well mounted. "They each had several horses," he says. "They would take their best horses to the junior rodeos. Seems like most every time they got home from a rodeo, Roy would be the first one to run in the house and show me what he won. A lot of times they'd get home from a rodeo, and there would be a 'play day' they wanted to go to around home. Those play days were sponsored by the Lee County Junior Rodeo Association, and they were just fun activities where the winners might get only $1.50 or $2.00 for each event. Roy always wanted to take his best horse to those things, and he'd get mad when I wouldn't let him. He didn't care what he won; he just wanted to win."

Roy was 14 when he lost a good horse named Brandy. Brandy had wandered into a cattle guard, and broke two legs while thrashing in a futile escape attempt before he was discovered. Roy cried and stayed behind while Tuffy hurried back out to put the horse down. "Roy was pretty tender-hearted," says Betty Rose. "He hated to see anything get hurt."

*Roy was 1973 NHSRA calf roping champ.*
**Photo by James Fain**

*Roping at the National High School Rodeo Association Finals in 1973 at Ogden, Utah.*
**Photo by James Fain**

**He rode his last bull when he was 15, and the ride placed first at the junior bull riding at Eunice, New Mexico.**

A horse named Beaver probably contributed more than any other to Roy's roping career when he was a teen-ager. Bill Murray called Tuffy from the Fort Worth rodeo and said he had found a good horse a kid could learn a lot on; he had navicular disease, but would probably last quite awhile with proper care. "Beaver really made Roy a roper," says Tuffy. "That horse would run hard, you could position him, use a jerk line on him. He'd limp back to the box after a run, but then he'd be ready to go again." Beaver is still around, retired on Roy's ranch at Durant, Oklahoma.

All the years Roy was growing, he concentrated on calf roping, mainly because Tuffy felt any other roping events, like team roping, would hurt his calf roping ability. But he did ride steers and bulls for several years at the junior rodeos, in addition to roping calves. When he was 12 or 13, he had the all-around saddle won at a rodeo—if he contested in at least one riding event, as the rules stipulated. Roy had drawn a Brangus bull that spooked him just a bit, and he considered just stepping off the bull once the gate opened. He wouldn't have to make a qualified ride in order to win the trophy saddle. But he went on to ride the bull, and took first in the event.

"I thought you were going to just step off," Tuffy said afterward.

"I was too scared to get off," Roy laughed.

He rode his last bull when he was 15, and the ride placed first at the junior bull riding at Eunice, New Mexico.

That was also the year he flanked a calf for the first time in competition—at the AJRA Finals. And he won the all-around award and opened his own bank account with $500. Aside from a few more horses supplied by Tuffy, Roy never needed any more money from home. When he was 16, he traded a couple saddles for an old pickup, and began rodeoing more and more on his own, throwing in with several slightly older rodeo hands who were cutting a wide swath through money at the area amateur rodeos.

Roy's only sport throughout high school was rodeo. He rodeoed a lot with Steve Bland, Byron Walker (who went on to win a PRCA steer wrestling world title), Kim Gripp, Jim Fuller, and Mac Altizer, rodeo notables all, and all at least second-generation cowboys. They listened endlessly to tapes by the rock group "Bad Company," en route to rodeos. And it got to a point where their cohesive club assumed the name Bad Company. Mac Altizer, son of past world champion Jim Bob Altizer, went on to become a rodeo stock contractor and even named his outfit Bad Company Rodeo.

Roy was president of AJRA his last year in the organization; and a photograph was taken of him kissing the new

*At the College National Finals Rodeo, 1975.*
**Photo by James Fain**

*National Finals Rodeo, 1982.*

**Photo by James Fain**

For Valentine's Day Lisa bought Roy a card that read: "I didn't marry you to change you . . . but don't be getting any worse!"

AJRA queen, Lisa Mann, his future wife. They were both 19.

Lisa had known Roy most of her life, because her family lives in Hobbs, and because she and her two brothers, Mike and Johnny, rodeoed in AJRA. Lisa competed in breakaway and ribbon roping, barrel racing, and pole bending. And she competed throughout college.

"Roy and I were just really good friends," says Lisa. "We went to different junior highs, but we were together in high school. I was a cheerleader, and I had a friend who was a cheerleader, and I'd get her dates with Roy. And Roy and I double-dated a lot. In college we started going together, and after a year or two we were married.

"Somehow it seems funny, marrying someone you grew up with, someone you've known all your life. My friends back home were sure surprised. I told them, 'Well, at least *I* won't be surprised with Roy, because I've known him all along.'" For Valentine's Day she bought Roy a card that read: *"I didn't marry you to change you...but don't be getting any worse!"*

Roy and Lisa went to college at Southeastern Oklahoma State University at Durant, and it's no secret that Roy, at least, was lured there in the first place by Dr. Leon Hibbs, the school president who was building a rodeo team at the time. Dr. Hibbs, with help from '73 PRCA calf roping champ Ernie Taylor, did put together a crack team, but always tried to instill in the rodeo students how important it was to prepare for a career once their rodeo days were over. Of Roy's classroom endeavor, Dr. Hibbs smiles and says, "Well, he attended, anyway." Roy was winning his first world championship in the PRCA at the time.

He also told Roy, "As long as you stay healthy, keep good horses, and continue to practice the way you do, there's no one in the world who will beat you—not day after day."

Roy and Lisa both liked the Durant area, and they bought their ranch just north of town. The herd of cows that runs on the place were all roping calves in years gone by. As the calves grew too big to rope, Roy selected the heifers he wanted to keep, and sold the others. The property is picturesque with woods and meadows. The house sits on a hill, and

the land slopes down to the Little Blue River. There's an indoor arena and an outdoor arena, barns and paddocks. Lisa's brother Johnny lives on the ranch, along with Kyle Stuart. Johnny and Kyle take care of the place while Roy is rodeoing.

"It's nice having them here," Lisa says. "They do the chores, and Roy doesn't have to worry about me and little Clint being alone while he's gone." Roy and Lisa's two-year-old son Clint likes to ride a spring-powered plastic Brahma in the house. He has his own hat, boots, and custom-made spurs; and shows regret over somehow being responsible for breaking the glass that covered a collection of Roy's trophy buckles. It's Clint who gets Roy out of bed in the morning, which is no small task, because Roy likes to sleep late when he's home.

Outside, Clint likes to wrestle with the cowdogs, two Blue Heelers named Coke and Forty. On their own time, Coke and Forty amuse themselves as most Blue Heelers do—by nipping at cattle and horses. "They've got some bad habits, but at least they're good with Clint," shrugs Lisa.

Roy bought a roping pony for Clint before Clint was even born. "I was pregnant when a boy who was 14 came to Roy's roping school with this pony. He was really too big for the pony, and Roy wound up buying him." Blair Burk, calf roper Barry Burk's son, is riding him for the time being. After all, Clint is only two years old.

But Roy acquired another pony, Bubba, who is also a Quarter pony trained for roping. Then last summer ('83) the family was in Durant for a carnival. Clint liked the pony ride, and Roy wound up paying the ride operator around $250 for a little Shetland mare named Buns. Unfortunately, Buns colicked and died a few months later.

"I cried and cried," Lisa said. "Roy said, 'Heck, I could lose a $10,000 rope horse and you wouldn't shed a tear. But you'll cry over a little carnival pony.' He told Clint, 'Buns died and Mommy cried.' So now Clint goes around saying, 'Buns died and Mommy cried.'"

In all probability, Clint will grow up roping. But Lisa has other things in mind as well: "I'd like to see him compete in other sports, too. And I want him to be a

*Roy, Clint, and Lisa, in the doorway to Roy's rodeo office.*

*Moms are handy for helping young cowboys
with their boots.*

*Clint bears down for a
ride on his Brahma,
provided by world
champion bull rider
Don Gay.*

ward to the National Finals Rodeo. "It's
exciting. And I'm just like all the other
rodeo wives there—I get nervous before
Roy competes."

Several years ago, she and Kyle ar-
rived home from a rodeo where they had
watched Roy. And while she may not re-
call exactly how Roy did at the contest,
she'll always remember that day as the
first time she saw the Little Blue River
suddenly become a big river that flowed
over the banks and flooded much of
their land.

"It hadn't even rained at home, but the
river started flooding about the time we
got there. We decided right quick to
move the cattle to higher ground; I went
out on foot while Kyle saddled a horse.
We cut the fence by the highway and
tried to get them up there, but they
wouldn't go, and pretty soon the water
was up to my shoulders. A neighbor
came by and said, 'Mrs. Cooper, you
ought to get out of there. I've seen three
or four water moccasins swim by.' I decided to get out."

They managed to save the cows by
turning out the roping calves on high
ground, where the cows could see them.
The cattle had to swim, but they made
it. "I tried to tell Roy about the flood,
but he wasn't impressed. He thought I
was exaggerating—until it flooded again
like that when he happened to be home."

Roy has grown to fully appreciate
Lisa, but the realization of just how important their marriage is to him didn't
occur until 1979, when Roy broke his
arm and his career was in jeopardy. "The
first couple years we were married, I was
just gone all the time. All I thought
about was rodeo and winning champi-
onships," he says. "It wasn't until I was
forced to stop—because my arm was in a
cast—that I realized how much Lisa
means to me, and how much help and
support she gives me. That's when we really got close."

The accident is still vivid in his mind.
He and Ernie Taylor were practicing at
Ernie's place. It was an indoor arena, it
had been raining that day, and the ropes
had some stiff spots in them because of
the variable temperature and humidity.
"Actually, we had quit roping; we were
done for the day. But one more calf ran
back up the alley and into the pen, and I
decided rather than turn him out, I'd go

good person; and to learn about the rest
of the world—not just the rodeo world."

Make no mistake, though; Lisa en-
joyed her own rodeo days, and wouldn't
mind competing again, locally: "Right
now, I'm content to stay home and take
care of Clint and Roy. And Roy is good
about coming home a lot. Most of the
year, he's here at least two or three days
a week."

Lisa is candid about the key to Roy's
continuous success in rodeo: "When he's
home, he's practicing. I've seen him
practice so long and so hard—so many
times—that he'll come to the house sick
to his stomach. A lot of people think
roping is something he just does naturally; they don't know how hard he
works at it.

"Roy talks about slowing down every
year. But he usually ends up going a little
harder than he did the previous year. He
talks like that when he's tired, but after
he's been home awhile, seen his family
and rested, then he gets restless. He has
to go again. He has it in him."

Lisa and Clint don't go with Roy to
many rodeos because, as she puts it,
"Having a family along slows down a rodeo cowboy." But Lisa really looks for-

ahead and rope him.

"I roped him real close and double-shuffled my slack—shot it up twice, and went to tag my horse. And stuck my hand right through a coil of that rope. It jerked me out of the saddle, and I was hung up. Finally my hand came loose and just hung there at a funny angle—and I knew...."

Roy told Ernie he wanted to go home. Ernie, fighting his own emotions, trying to stay calm in light of the very real prospect that Roy's roping career might have just ended, told him, "No, I think we better get you to a doctor."

Roy wound up in a Dallas hospital, where he stayed for eight days while doctors pinned and cast his wrist and forearm. He had 92 phone calls from well-wishers the first day, though he talked to no one. And the calls continued after he was released from the hospital. "Seems like all the ropers called me, encouraging me."

Despite being out of competition for more than two months at the height of the season, Roy managed to qualify for the Finals that year. "I knew I couldn't try to be real fast and win any go-rounds, because my wrist was too stiff—it still had the pins in it. All I wanted to do at the NFR was tie down all my calves and hope to place well in the average." What he did was tie down all his calves and set a new fast-time record for the NFR average: 107.9 seconds on ten calves.

"When I won the National Finals that year, it probably meant more to me than being world champion the first year. When I started roping again, after the accident, I realized how much I love to rope, how much I had missed it. I'll always rope because of the feeling it gives me. When I rope—when I make a good run—I feel like I'm winning."

And he is.

**He set a new fast-time record for the NFR average: 107.9 seconds on ten calves.**

*Roy likes to sleep late when he gets the chance. It takes Clint to get him out of bed.*

# 12 CALF ROPING RULES

**Refer to the latest PRCA rule book for any changes in rules and regulations.**

Reprinted from the PRCA rule book with permission of Professional Rodeo Cowboys Association, 101 Prorodeo Dr., Colorado Springs, Colo. 80919.

Rope may be dallied or tied hard and fast; either is permissible. Contestant must rope calf, dismount, go down rope and throw calf by hand, and cross and tie any three (3) feet. To qualify as a legal tie, there shall be at least one (1) wrap around all three legs, and a half-hitch. If calf is down when roper reaches it, the calf must be let up to his feet and be thrown by hand. If roper's hand is on the calf when calf falls, calf is considered thrown by hand. Rope must hold calf until roper gets hand on calf. Tie must hold, and three legs remained crossed, until passed on by the judge; and roper must not touch calf after giving "finished" signal until after judge has completed his examination. The field flag judge will pass on the tie of calves through use of a stopwatch, timing six (6) seconds from the time the rope horse takes his first step forward after the roper has remounted. Rope will not be removed from calf, and rope must remain slack until field judge has passed on tie. In the event a contestant's catch rope is off a calf after completion of tie, the six-second time period is to start when roper clears calf. Flagger must watch calf during the six-second period and will stop watch when a calf kicks free, using the time shown on the watch to determine whether calf was tied long enough to qualify. Roper will be disqualified for removing rope from calf after signaling for time, until the tie has been passed on by the field judge. If tie comes loose, or calf gets to his feet before tie has been ruled a fair one, the roper will be marked "no time."

Two loops will be permitted, catch-as-catch-can, and should the roper miss with both, he must retire and no time will be allowed. Roping calf without releasing loop from hand is not permitted. If roper intends to use two loops, he must carry two (2) ropes, and must use second rope for second loop. There will be a thirty-five-second (35-second) elapsed time limit in the calf roping. A whistle indicating "no time" shall be blown by the timer at the end of the 35-second span. Deviations must be approved by the Calf Roping Director.

Contestant must adjust rope and reins in a manner that will prevent horse from dragging calf. Contestant must receive no assistance of any kind from outside. If horse drags calf excessively, field judge may stop horse and a penalty not to exceed a one-hundred-dollar ($100) fine may be assessed by the field flag judge and/or any director.

The line judge in the calf roping event should stand on the opposite side of the chute that the contestants are competing from. This pertains to all rodeos that use an automatic barrier. For rodeos where a hand-pulled barrier is used, the decision of lining calves still must be made by the Calf Roping Director, or a director assistant in that event.

Automatic barrier must be used at all rodeos for calf roping. At indoor rodeos, length of score will be determined by arena conditions. The minimum length of score at outdoor rodeos will be the length of the roping box minus four (4) feet. The maximum length of score, when automatic barrier is used, will be eighteen (18) feet. All score lengths are subject to Calf Roping Director's or representative's approval.

If there must be a rerun of calves to complete a go-round, all calves must be tied down before any stock is drawn. If, after one (1) go-round has been completed, a fresh calf has to be used, the calf must be roped and tied before the drawing; but if extra calves have been tied at that rodeo, they will not be considered fresh.

# 13 CALF ROPING TERMINOLOGY

**Here it is, from A to "V."**

AVERAGE—Competitions with more than one go-round pay prize money for each round, plus money for the best average, or total time. The winner of the average is the overall winner of the contest.

BARRIER—The rope that is stretched across the front of the box from which the roper emerges at the start of a calf roping run. If the roper rides through the rope and breaks the barrier before the calf has tripped the release mechanism, the contestant receives a ten-second penalty. The Hallettsville automatic barrier is the most popular in use.

BOX—The area along the side of the chute, where horse and rider stand, ready to rope.

BURNER—The small piece of leather or rawhide laced on the honda of a rope to prevent the honda from wearing out.

CHUTE—The small enclosure from which the calf is released into the arena.

CURL—Refers to the upward curling action of a loop as it encircles the calf's neck. A good curl indicates the loop has been thrown well.

ENTRY FEE—The amount of money a contestant pays to enter a competition. Entry fees are pooled to form prize money. At all PRCA rodeos, and some individual ropings, the fees are also added to purse money to form total prize money.

FLANKING—Grasping the catch rope next to the calf's neck with one hand, and reaching across the calf's back to grasp his flank with the other hand in order to pick him up and lay him down on his side, in preparation for the tie.

GO-ROUND—Also referred to as "round." A competition will have at least one go-round; a go-round is complete when every contestant has competed once.

HONDA—The eye in one end of the rope. The other end of the rope is passed through the honda to form a loop.

HOOEY—A slang term in roping; a hooey is the half-hitch put in the piggin' string, completing the tie.

JACKPOT—A competition in which only entry fees are pooled for prize money. No purse money is added.

JERK—Refers to the abrupt contact by means of the rope between calf and horse, when the horse stops the calf.

JERK LINE—The jerk line is a long soft rope attached to the bridle bit, passed through a ring or pulley attached to the saddle swell, and tucked in the roper's belt. The rope pulls free from the roper as he runs to the calf, and in the process, helps signal the horse to back a step or two and keep the rope tight.

LAP-AND-TAP—A roping competition that is run without using a barrier.

LEGGING—Lifting a calf's front leg, tipping him to his side in preparation for the tie. This is an alternative to flanking.

NECK ROPE—In reference to a horse, this is the rope that encircles his neck, halfway between his head and withers. The tail of the catch rope is passed through the neck rope and attached to the saddle horn. This keeps the horse straight with the roped calf; it prevents the horse from turning away while the roper is flanking and tying.

PIGGING STRING—Usually pronounced "piggin' string"; a length of twisted nylon, with a loop in one end, used to tie three legs on a calf.

PULLING SLACK—The act of grasping the rope with a hand after the loop has settled on the target, and pulling, thereby taking the "slack" out of the rope and tightening the loop. Synonymous terms include "grabbing slack" or "jerking slack."

RATE—A good roping horse should rate calves to afford the roper his best throw. A horse does this by moving into the correct position behind the calf, and maintaining an even speed with the calf while the rider swings his loop and prepares to throw.

SCORE—This word has a couple of meanings, according to the context in which it is used. It may refer to the length of head start given a calf from the chute to the score line (perhaps 8 to 15 feet or more, depending on individual arena conditions). Or it may refer to the horse-training procedure whereby the horse is held in the box while a calf is released from the chute, but the roper prevents the horse from pursuing the calf. This teaches the horse not to anticipate, and to leave the box only when the roper signals him to leave. A good rope horse should "score well."

SPOKE—The section or length of rope not in the loop, but held next to the loop, between the honda and the roper's hand.

THE TIE—Refers to placing three of the calf's legs together and wrapping the piggin' string around them, then securing the string with a half-hitch.

THE V—The imaginary letter formed by placing the calf's legs together in preparation for the tie.

# NOTE ON THE PHOTOGRAPHY

**A fresh and graphic insight into the way champions work.**

All instructional photographs in this book, to include the pictures on the front and back covers, were made with two Pentax LXs, one armed with the pistol-grip-type motor drive, the other with a battery-powered winder. Two lenses were used throughout: SMC Pentax-M 80-200mm f4.5 and Pentax SMC-M 35-70mm f3.5. The films were Tri-X (developed in HC110) and Kodachrome 64, both manufactured by Kodak.

The Pentax LX with motor drive is an ideal camera for this kind of photography. The long grip makes the camera easy to hold, and the trigger at the top of the grip allows you to focus with one hand and squeeze off the shutter with the other. Because of the streamlined shape and positioning of the grip, vertical compositions can be shifted to quickly and effortlessly. The five-frames-per-second speed of the motor-driven LX is a necessity when you want to break down the action of a fast calf roping run by the likes of a Roy Cooper.

A self-propelled platform (equipped with a scissors lift) was employed frequently to get a view often not seen, either from a spectator's or participant's perspective. This overhead look has become an important facet of the *Western Horseman's* new series of instruction books, and it has given a fresh and graphic insight into the way champions work.

*—KURT MARKUS*

*Pentax LX 35mm SLR with motor drive.*

*Pentax LX 35mm SLR with motor drive (powered by penlight batteries in the grip).*

*Roy Cooper (left) and Kurt Markus aloft on the scissors-lift platform.*

# ACKNOWLEDGEMENT

Special thanks to the crew who worked behind the scenes—Johnny Mann, Clay Cooper, and Kyle Stuart—who penned calves, opened gates, untied calves, and lended a hand wherever needed. Pictured with Roy are Johnny and Kyle (front), Clay, and Randy Witte.

—RANDY WITTE & KURT MARKUS

## Western Horseman Magazine

*Colorado Springs, Colorado*

The Western Horseman Magazine, established in 1936, is the world's leading horse publication. For subscription information and a list of other Western Horseman books, contact: Western Horseman Magazine, Box 7980, Colorado Springs, CO 80933-7980; ph. 719-633-5524.

Distributed to the book trade by
Gulf Publishing Company
Box 2608, Houston, TX 77252-2608
Ph. 713-520-4444